400 GREATEST

JOKES

**For Investment Advisors,
Financial Planners,
Financial Speakers,
Insurance Agents,
CPAs, Bankers,
& Stockbrokers**

Larry Klein
CPA/PFS, MBA
Certified Senior Advisor

NF Communications, Inc.
1700 N Broadway #405, Walnut Creek, CA 94596
800-980-0192, www.nfcom.com

Some of the jokes in this book were excerpted from the following:
A FUNNY THING HAPPENED ON THE WAY TO THE PODIUM
by Herbert V. Prochnow, copyright © 1998, 2000 by Herbert
Prochnow. Used by permission of Prima Publishing, a division of
Random House, Inc.

SPEAKERS LIBRARY OF BUSINESS STORIES, ANECDOTES
AND HUMOR
by Joe Griffith copyright © 1990.
Reprinted with permission of Prentice Hall Direct.

Introduction

I went through over 6,000 jokes to find these best 400.

A word of caution: Humor is a personal thing. You have, of course, noticed that some things that make you laugh, other people think are stupid; other people like your wife. (Ladies, you already have a good sense of humor, so my comments are directed at the men).

So be prepared to think that half of these jokes are stupid. These are the ones your spouse will urge you to tell at your next seminar because they're "cute." But a 50% "funny ratio" is pretty good because 95% of the jokes in the world are really bad. In fact, if you find one dozen jokes that you really like, you've hit pay dirt. I have used the same six jokes for my entire seminar-giving career and the audience gets a good laugh every time.

Almost every joke can be told in mixed company, and are great for using in seminars and presentations. There are, however, a few that are best left as one-to-one stories for your closer clients.

Let me spend a little time on the issue of delivery by stating that there is no funny joke. The funniness is in the *way* you tell the joke. Every salesperson gets introduced to this model early in their career:

Effectiveness of Communication

What You Say	7%
How You Say It	38%
Body Language	55%

Body language is so important that, if you were here with me now, without saying a word I could start dancing and make you laugh. Believe me, watching me dance is funny. Good joke telling is not in the joke, it's in the telling.

Here are three rules for telling a joke well:

1. Your descriptions must paint a picture:

Weak: "This short guy walks into a bar..."

Strong: "This tiny, little guy walks into a bar. He's so short that, when he raises his hands over his head (you raise your hands over your head as you say this), you still can't see him over the table."

2. You must step into the shoes of the characters in the joke and alternate between narrator and characters:

Weak: "So he walks up to the bar and asks for a drink in a high voice."

Strong: "So he walks up to the bar and says, in a high, squeaky voice, "Can I have a drink?" (as *you* squeak in a high voice).

3. And the most important part: you must act out the joke with your body. For example, when you are the tiny guy asking for the drink, you put your hands up to your chin like you're straining to speak over the edge of the bar, and you look up as though you are talking to the 6 foot tall bartender (and you are 4 feet tall).

Learning these three tactics is easy with a little practice. Read the book and circle your favorite jokes. Then, practice telling these in front of your spouse, your best critic. This will be the best test as your spouse won't like the jokes you select, but if s/he says you told it well, you've got a winner. (By the way, if you're waiting for the punch line about this little guy with the high voice in the bar, I don't know any joke like that.)

This book comes with an audio CD which gives you some additional examples of good joke telling. That way, if you illegally copied this book thinking you were going to save a few dollars, all I've got to say is, "Sorry, you cheap bastard."

The good thing is, there's an order form in the back and you can get a paid copy of the book with the audio CD and redeem yourself in this world.

Thank you and good laughing!

Table of Contents

Aging

All of my marketing is for seniors. Some jokes may not relate to financial topics, but they are useful for building rapport. For example, sometimes I will ask the audience, "Does anyone here ever have the experience of not remembering things?" They all nod like mad in agreement.

I can then launch into a joke, "That reminds me of the gentleman who...." Since so much financial advising is related to retirement planning or retirement investing, aging jokes often fit nicely.

A man goes to heaven and he's asked what he would like to do. "I love golf!" he says.

"Okay," says St. Peter, "here's a set of clubs and our most experienced caddy. He's 118 years old."

"118 years old!" protests the man. "How good can he be?"

"His eyesight is incredible. Hit the ball as far as you can and he'll see it."

They get up to the first tee and the man, an experienced golfer, whacks the ball 350 yards.

He turns to the caddy. "Did you see it?" he asks.

"Sure did," says the caddy.

"Where is it?" asks the man

Caddy says, "I forget."

An example that everything is not as it seems on the surface (e.g., a widely-advertised mutual fund that people think is good, but a closer look shows it lags the market considerably). That reminds me of the time...:

A retired gentleman returns home from golf. He's been concerned about his wife losing her hearing, so he decides to test it.

From the living room, he hollers to her in the kitchen, "Honey, what's for dinner?" No reply.

He moves closer, into the dining room and again says a little louder, "Honey, what's for dinner?" Again, no reply.

So he walks into the kitchen and stands three feet behind his wife and repeats, "Honey, what's for dinner?"

She turns around with a perturbed look on her face, "Harry, for the third time, roast beef and mashed potatoes!"

Three retirees, each with a hearing loss, were taking a walk one fine March day.

One remarked to the other, "Windy, ain't it?"

"No," the second man replied, "it's Thursday."

The third man chimed in, "So am I. Let's have a Coke."

My grandfather got a new hearing aid last week and he showed it to me. I asked, "What kind is it?"

He answered, "A quarter 'til three."

A fellow went to the doctor who told him that he had a bad illness and only one year to live.

So, he decided to talk to his pastor. After the man explained his situation, he asked his pastor if there was anything he could do.

"What you should do is go out and buy a late '70s or early '80s model Dodge pickup," said the pastor. "Then go get married to the ugliest woman you can find, and buy yourselves an old trailer house in the panhandle of Oklahoma."

The fellow asked, "Will this help me live longer?"

"No," said the pastor, "but it will make what time you do have seem like forever."

I recently received a phone call from one of my longtime clients, a man who's in his late 80s.

Just into the conversation, I said, "So, what's new?"

He said, "Actually, I just got married!"

I said, "That's great! Congratulations, you sly fox. So tell me about her, is she a great cook, or what?"

He said, "No, she can't cook to save her life."

I said, "Okay, well, that's not important, you've got lots of great places to eat near you. Well, she must be a real cutie pie, huh?"

He said, "No, actually, that's not one of her strong points, either."

So I said, "I'll bet she's a real romantic type, lots of hugs and kisses, eh?" Again, he said, "No, she's not particularly affectionate, my friend."

At that point I had to say, "Hold on! We've known each other for a really long time, and now you get married. You tell me your wife can't cook, she's not much of a looker, and she's basically kind of a cold fish! Why in the world did you marry her?"

He was quiet for a minute, and then he said, "Frankly, out of all the people my age around me, she's the only one who has her driver's license!"

A man says to his wife, "It's my sixty-fifth birthday today. I'm going down to the Social Security office to apply for benefits."

His wife says, "Take some form of identification like a drivers license or birth certificate."

The man says, "I don't need any of that stuff. See you later." He comes back several hours later.

His wife says, "So, what happened?"

The man says, "What do you mean 'what happened?' I went and got my Social Security."

The wife says, "How did you get Social Security without proving your age?"

The man says, "Well, I went up to the young lady and unbuttoned my shirt and showed her my white chest hair, and she gave me my Social Security."

Wife says excitedly, "Well, you old coot, while you were there you should have dropped your drawers and applied for total disability!"

Continue to make money in retirement...

This just in ...Officials in Washington have announced that the retirement age will increase from 65 to 67, initially affecting people born in 1938. And you know what that means...yet one MORE tour by the Rolling Stones.

An older woman was losing her hearing. A surgeon she consults tells her that ear transplants are still in the testing stage, but he will do what he can.

The woman undergoes the operation, and after a time she returns to the surgeon's office to have the bandages removed and the stitches taken out. After examining her, the doctor tells her everything seems to have gone well, and she seems pleased with his work.

The next day, however, she calls the plastic surgeon in a rage.

"You know what you did?" she screams. "You gave me a man's ears."

"Well," says the surgeon, "an ear is an ear. What's wrong?

Can't you hear?"

"I hear everything," she says. "The problem is I don't understand anything I'm told."

How many of you think that you've gotten physically stronger the last 10 years? NO? Well, you have, and I can prove it to you.

When you went to the store 10 years ago, you could probably carry $20 worth of groceries all by yourself…I'll bet that today you can carry about $40 worth of groceries all by yourself!

Living Longer...

Mr. Johnson goes to the Doctor for a physical. Doc says, "Mr. Johnson, you are in great shape for a man your age."

Mr. Johnson replies, "How old do you think I am?"

"About 65 or so." says the Doc.

"I am 82 years old."
"Wow!" says the Doc." Your Father must have been very old when he died."

"What makes you think that he's dead?"

"He's not?" said the doctor.

"No, he is healthy, 103 years old, and lives with my mom in Florida."

"WOW!" says the doctor again. Then your grandfather must have been *very* old when he died."

"What makes you think that *he* is dead?"

"He's not?!" replied the doctor.

"Heck no, he's 125 years old, very healthy and, in fact, he will be moving into a new house next weekend."

"Why would he move now?" said the startled doctor.

"Well," said Mr. Johnson, "His parents finally decided that he had to get his own place."

A little old lady seated herself right behind the bus driver. Every ten minutes or so she'd pipe up, "Have we reached Oriskany Falls yet, Sonny?"

"No, lady, not yet. I'll let you know," he replied, time after time. The hours passed, the old woman kept asking for Oriskany Falls, and finally the little town came into view.

Sighing with relief, the driver pulled over and called out, "This is where you get out, lady."

"Is this Oriskany Falls?"

"YES!" he bellowed. "Get out!"

"Oh, I'm going all the way to Albany, Sonny," she explained sweetly. "It's just that my daughter told me that when we got this far, I should take my first blood pressure pill."

Dear Pastor:

I, myself, have become quite a frivolous old gal since I wrote you last. As a matter of fact, I'm seeing five different gentleman everyday.

When I get up in the morning, Will Power gets me out of bed. Then I immediately go see John. A few minutes later, Charley Horse comes along. When he leaves, Arthur-itis shows up and, finally, I'm so tired, I go to bed with Ben Gay.

It is well-documented that for every minute you exercise, you add one minute to your life. This enables you, at 85 years old, to spend an additional five months in a nursing home at $10,000 per month.

A matronly lady walks into her broker's office with her statement in her hand. She asks, "Is this stock you recommended ever going to come back?"

"Absolutely," her broker says, "it has great earnings and a fine management team."

"Is it going to come back in my lifetime?" she asks.

"Well, frankly, Mrs. Smith, I wish you were a lot younger."

So what do you call it when you have a bagel, cream cheese, coffee and a diaper?

Incontinental breakfast.

I was reading an article just the other day that stated, "With just a few minor medical breakthroughs, it won't be uncommon for us to live past the age of 100!"

I told this to a client of mine and he kinda frowned. I asked, "Aren't you excited about the prospect of living to age 100?"

He looked at me and said, "Living to 100 would be great, it's the thought of my 75-year-old son wanting to move back in with me that scares me."

I tell this one to demonstrate the need for long-term care...

Many people ask me "How do you live in an area with so many retirees—they are such bad drivers!"

"The problem is not the bad driving of retirees, but that of their parents!"

An old, rich man is having his 90th birthday party and his sons want to get him something special.

So, they have a banquet catered and hire a a gorgeous woman to serve his every desire.

She saunters up to the old man and asks, "Would you like super sex?"

The man replies, "I'll take the soup."

As a senior citizen was driving down the freeway, his car phone rang.

Answering, he heard his wife's voice urgently warning him,

"Herman, I just heard on the news that there's a car going the wrong way on 280. Please be careful!"

"Hell," said Herman, "It's not just one car. It's hundreds of them!"

To Exercise or Not To Exercise...

I joined a health club last year, spent about $400. Haven't lost a pound. Apparently you have to show up.

I have to exercise early in the morning before my brain figures out what I am doing.

I don't exercise at all. If God meant us to touch our toes, he would have put them further up our body.

I like long walks, especially when they are taken by people who annoy me.

I have flabby thighs, but, fortunately, my stomach covers them.

The advantage of exercising every day is that you die healthier.

If you are going to try cross-country skiing, start with a small country.

Banks/Banking

A well-dressed gentleman enters Citibank's main office in New York and applies for a $100 loan, which he says he needs for his vacation to Europe. Although the bank does not normally make such small loans, he is a large depositor with the bank and the loan officer has him complete the application.

The loan office explains that the bank's policy is to have some outside collateral. The gentleman offers his Rolls-Royce and points to it in the bank parking lot.

One month later he returns to pay off his loan, a total of $125 with interest and fees.

The loan officer cannot help but ask, "Mr. Smith, you have been a large depositor with us. Why did you want a loan for $100?"

"It wasn't so much the loan I wanted. Where else could I park my car in Manhattan for an entire month for $25?"

David Letterman's ***Top Ten Signs You're Doing Business With The Wrong Bank***
As presented on the 3/7/95 broadcast of
The Late Show with David Letterman

10. When you make a deposit, tellers high-five each other.

9. After you get a free toaster, bank president shows up at your house begging for toast.

8. Your monthly statements are handwritten, in crayon.

7. When you want to make a withdrawal, clerks suddenly don't speak English.

6. You notice Kato Kaelin is sleeping in the vault.

5. Your safety deposit box is a Dunkin' Donuts carton wrapped in tinfoil.

4. All cash deposits go directly into teller's pants.

3. Lobby is waist-deep in Mexican pesos.

2. Toll-free customer service line is: 1-800-GET-HOSED.

1. Four words: Bank President Rosa Lopez.

Five signs that maybe your bank isn't on the level:

1. The bank president is Roger Clinton.
2. All the bank tellers are wearing "I'm with Stupid" T-shirts.
3. When you open a new account, they give you a set of dishes that say, "Property of Airport Marriott."
4. When cashing a check, instead of dollars they give you handfuls of smooth pebbles.
5. They give you personal checks with the words "Insufficient Funds" pre-stamped on the front.

One January, when the bank was in the midst of its renewal season, one of the bank customers came to review the results of his past year.

They talked about cattle first. "Well," the farmer said, "we had some tough weather during calving, and the new herd came up short. Then, with the dry weather through the summer, pastures were weak and the calves didn't gain well. In the end, we lost money on the cattle — but it could be worse."

Hoping to find a better topic, the banker moved on to questions about the hog enterprise. "The hogs looked mighty good this year."

Replied the farmer, "But then we found a problem with rhinitis in the nursery, and that slowed the pigs to market.

Turns in the farrowing shed were slow because of problems in the rations, and the markets declined with poor exports and a strong dollar overseas. In the end, we lost money on the hogs — but it could be worse."

By now, the banker was running out of hope, but he proceeded to ask about crops.

"Well you know the corn was poor this year because of the hail in the spring and a dry summer," began the farmer, "but the soybeans looked good until the nematodes showed up. We had a nice hay crop, but sold it to make your land payment before the market really took off in the Fall. I can't see how we are going to avoid losing money on the crops, too — but hey, it could be worse."

At this point, the banker had heard all he could stand. "What do you mean 'it could be worse?'" the banker exploded, "you've lost money on every part of your business this year! How could it be any worse?"

The farmer paused a moment, and with grim irony, said "Well, it could have been *my* money!"

According to inside contacts, the Japanese banking crisis shows no signs of ameliorating. If anything, it's getting worse.

Following last week's news that Origami Bank had folded, we are hearing that Sumo Bank has gone belly up and

Bonsai Bank plans to cut back some of its branches. Karaoke Bank is up for sale and is (you guessed it!) going for a song.

Meanwhile, shares in Kamikaze Bank have nose-dived and 500 back-office staff at Karate Bank got the chop. Analysts report that there is something fishy going on at Sushi Bank and the staff there fear they may get a raw deal.

When Things Go Wrong

A good story during a bear market. How many people are a little dismayed with how your investments are doing right now? Let me share with you the words of a very famous person...

When John Glenn was all suited up, ready to go on his first space mission, a reporter walked up, put a microphone in his face and asked, "What happens if your rockets don't fire when you're ready to come back?"

John Glenn replied, "It'll ruin my day."

Unlike John Glenn, you have time to enjoy better days.

Upon John Glenn's successful return, the same reporter greeted him and asked, "What were you thinking about when you were coming down?"

John Glenn replies, "That this capsule was manufactured by the lowest bidder."

Bear markets even affect the moods of little schoolchildren...

A first grade teacher had a small number of children gathered around a table for a reading group. After the story was read, she gave the children a worksheet to do. She thought they may have some trouble with it, so she wanted them to work on it right then.

She heard a little girl named Mary softly say, "Damn!"

The teacher leaned over and said quietly to little Mary, "We don't say that in school, Mary."

Little Mary looked at the teacher with her eyes very big and innocent and she said, "Not even when things have all gone to Hell?!"

Did you hear about the banker who was arrested for embezzling $100,000 to pay for his daughter's college education?

As the policeman, who also had a daughter in college, was leading him away in handcuffs, he asks, "I have just one question for you. Where were you going to get the *rest* of the money?"

For your prospects who use the discount broker, who are do-it-yourselfers, or want the no-load item. Read this aloud to an audience:

Dear Sir,

I'm writing in response to your request for additional information.

In block #3 of the accident report form, I put "Trying to do the job alone" as the cause of the accident. In your letter you said that I should explain more fully and I trust that the following details should be sufficient.

I'm a bricklayer by trade. On the date of the accident, I was working alone on the roof of a new three-story building. When I completed my work, I discovered I had about 300 pounds of brick left over. Rather than carry the bricks down by hand I decided to lower them in a barrel by using a pulley that was attached to the side of the building at the third floor. Securing the rope at ground level I went to the roof, swung the barrel out and loaded the bricks into it. Then I went back to the ground and untied the rope while holding it tightly to ensure a slow descent of the three hundred pounds of bricks.

You will note in block #2 of the accident report form that I stated I weighed 165 pounds. Due to my surprise at being jerked off the ground so suddenly, I lost my presence of mind and did not let go of the rope. Needless to say, I proceeded at a rather rapid rate up the side of the building. In the middle of the second floor, I met the barrel coming down. This explains the fractured skull and broken collarbone.

Slowed down only slightly by the barrel, I continued my rapid ascent, not stopping until my right hand was two knuckles deep into the pulley. Fortunately, I retained consciousness and was able to hold tightly to the rope in spite of my pain and injuries.

At approximately the same time, however, the barrel of bricks hit the ground and the bottom of the barrel broke out. Devoid of the weight of the bricks, the barrel weighed approximately 50 pounds. I refer you again to my weight in box #2. I began a rather rapid descent down the side of the building. In the middle of the second floor, I again met the barrel coming up. This accounts for my two fractured ankles and lacerations of my legs and lower body. This encounter with the barrel slowed me enough to lessen injuries when I fell onto the pile of bricks. Fortunately, only three vertebrae were cracked.

I'm sorry to report, however, as I lay there on the bricks, in pain, unable to stand or move, I lost my presence of mind and let go of the rope. The empty barrel, weighing more than the rope, came back down and broke both of my legs.

I hope I have furnished the information that you need to complete the processing of my claim and that you understand how the accident occurred by trying to do the job alone.

Sincerely,
S. Anderson

Deduction...

Sherlock Holmes and Dr. Watson were on a camping trip.

They had gone to bed and were lying there looking up at the sky. Holmes said, "Watson, look up. What do you see?"

"Well, I see thousands of stars."

"And what does that mean to you?"

"Well, I guess it means we will have another nice day tomorrow. What does it mean to you, Holmes?"

"To me, it means someone has stolen our tent."

A man walks into a bar and asks the bartender to quickly pour him a drink before the trouble starts.

The bartender pours the man a drink and watched as the man drank it and said, "Give me another drink before the trouble starts."

The bartender gives him another drink and the man drinks it down as quickly as the first.

After several rounds of this the bartender said to the man, "Look buddy, you have been in here 10 minutes and you keep talking about the trouble starting. Just when is the trouble going to start?"

The man looks at him and says, "The trouble starts just as soon as you find out that I ain't got any money."

Procrastination...

Mother says to her son, "Get up and go to school, you'll be late."

The son whines, "But mom, all the kids call me names and none of the teachers like me."

The mother says, "I'll give you two good reasons why you're gonna get out of this bed and go to school right now. First, you're 35 years old! Second, you're the principal!"

A yuppie opened the door of his BMW, when suddenly a car came along and hit the door, ripping it off completely.

When the police arrived at the scene, the yuppie was complaining bitterly about the damage to his precious BMW.

"Officer, look what they've done to my Beeemer!" He whined.

"You yuppies are so materialistic, you make me sick!" retorted the officer. "You're so worried about your stupid BMW, that you didn't even notice that your left arm was ripped off!

"Oh my GAWD!" the yuppie cried, "Where's my Rolex?!"

The Zen master steps up to the hot dog stand and says, "Make me one with everything."

The hot dog vendor fixes a hot dog and hands it to the Zen master, who pays with a $20 bill. The hot dog vendor puts the bill in the cash drawer and closes it.

"Where's my change?" asks the Zen master.

The hot dog vendor responds, "Change must come from within."

Doctors

I personally find lawyer jokes tiring and most of them boring and far too critical. Most people can, however, relate well to doctor jokes, especially retirees. Any of these jokes can be started off by saying, "Has anyone here been to the doctor lately?"

A man told his doctor that he wasn't able to do all the things around the house that he used to do. When the examination was complete, he said, "Now, Doc, I can take it. Tell me in plain English what is wrong with me."

"Well, in plain English," the doctor replied, "you're just lazy."

"Okay," said the man. "Now give me the medical term so I can tell my wife."

"Mr. Clark, I'm afraid I have bad news," the doctor told his anxious patient. "You only have six months to live."

The man sat in stunned silence for the next several minutes.

Regaining his composure, he apologetically told his physician that he had no medical insurance. "I can't possibly pay you in that time," he says.

"Okay," the doctor said. "Let's make it nine months."

A man goes into the hospital for some tests. The medical staff knocks him out, and when he comes around, there is a doctor peering over him pulling up his eyelid and wielding the reflex hammer.

The doctor says, "I'm glad you're awake. I'm afraid I have some mixed news."

The man says, "Don't hold back, Doc, tell me the bad news."

The doctor says, "It was worse than we thought; we had to amputate your left leg."

The man then asks, "What is the good news then?"

The doctor replies, "The man in the next bed wants to buy your slippers."

An agitated patient was stomping around the psychiatrist's office, running his hands through his hair, almost in tears.

"Doctor, my memory's gone. Gone! I can't remember my wife's name. Can't remember my children's names. Can't remember what kind of car I drive. Can't remember where I work. It was all I could do to find my way here!"

"Calm down. How long have you been like this?"

"Like what?"

A man walks into a doctor's office. He has a cucumber up his nose, a carrot in his left ear and a banana in his right ear.

"What's the matter with me?" he asks the doctor.

The doctor replies, "You're not eating properly."

Patient after a physical, "Well, Doc, how do I stand?"

Doctor: "I don't know, it's a miracle to me!"

"Doctor, Doctor, you must help me! My husband thinks he's a dog!"

Doctor: "How long has this been going on?"

"Ever since he was a puppy!"

Naked woman to a naked man in the doctor's waiting room:

"That doctor is a little strange. I've just got a broken finger, and he made me take all my clothes off."

"I know what you mean," replied the naked man. "I came here to fix the radiator."

On speaking about health care being too expensive:

"My doctor sure got me on my feet again. His bill was so high, I had to sell my car."

My doctor has never violated his oath—the oath he took years ago to become a millionaire.

Doing Stupid Things

A farmer wins $1 million in the lottery. The newspaper reporter comes to interview him. "What are you going to do with the money?"

The farmer replies, "I'll just keep farming until it's all gone."

Some people are reading the wrong things and getting financial advice from the wrong people. Talk about looking in the wrong places — reminds me of my friend who went ice fishing.

He had never done it before. He went out with his ax and his auger to drill through the ice.

He arrives at a spot and starts drilling. A few minutes go by and he hears a booming voice from above. "There's no fish under that ice."

Terrified and in a sheepish voice, he asks, "Who's that speaking?" (as you look up toward the ceiling with a frightened look.)

"The Ice Rink Manager."

Aspiring investor to Investment Counselor: "I'm drawing 10% interest on money in my savings account."

Investment Counselor: "Hmmm, that's interesting! The best I've seen is 5% on savings accounts."

Aspiring Investor: "I beat the system! I put half my cash in one bank at 5%, and half in another bank at another 5%!"

Speaking about financial mistakes reminds me of the Pope on his birthday.

His aides asked him what he would like to do on his birthday and he says, "I want to drive the limousine today." They say okay.

They jump in the back seat, and the Pope jumps behind the wheel and takes off down the narrow streets of Rome. Having not driven much, he's bumping into buildings and knocking over fruit stands and is soon pulled over by the police.

The policeman calls into the sergeant and says, "Sergeant, I think I have made a big mistake by pulling over a very important person."

"Is it the magistrate?"

"No." replies the officer.

"Is it the mayor?" Asks the sergeant.
"No, he's much more important." says the officer.

"Is it Tony Bennett or Wayne Newton?"

"No," says the officer, "He's much more important. This guy has the Pope for a driver!"

I am always amazed at how journalists always have a reason for why the stock market went up or down...

In fact, they just about make up reasons. It reminds me of the two guys approaching each other on the sidewalk, and both are dragging their right foot as they walk.

As they meet, one looks at the other knowingly, points to his right foot and says, "Land mine, Vietnam, 1969."

The other hooks his thumb over his shoulder and says, "Dog poop. 20 feet back. Look out."

This story is just to remind you that no one knows why the market goes up or down today or tomorrow. The key is to have a plan over time and stick with it (or you may get the same result the second guy got in our story).

Do you have any friends that boast about some investment they made and how much money they made? Don't feel bad — these are the same people who never tell you about the losers. They don't tell you what really happened.

It's like the cleaning crew in the lobby of an impressive hotel. They cleaned around a guest who had obviously imbibed a bit much. He was sprawled across several chairs, his clothes were in disarray, and he was moaning gently.

They went on and cleaned the rest of the hotel, and as they were ending their shift eight hours later, one of the crew (his name was Joe) noticed the drunk hadn't moved. Joe thought about it and decided to check further. He went to the man and nudged him a bit. The man moaned.

Joe asked, "Hey, man, how long you been here?"

The man moaned some more, obviously in great pain, and mumbled, "Since last night."

Joe, thinking he should get the man to his room, asked, "Hey, where you from?"

The man moaned again, and croaked, "From the balcony."

Don't make any assumptions about how others are doing with investments until you hear the WHOLE story.

A man found himself talking with God:

Man: "God, how much is a million years to you?"

God: "Oh, about a second..."

Man: "God, how much is a million dollars to you?"

God: "Oh, about a penny..."

Man: "Wow! God, will you give me a million dollars?"

God: "In a second..."

I once told a woman I charged 1% annually to manage her portfolio. She thought that was too high because she told me her mutual fund cost her nothing.

So I told her how to save a lot with a story of a man who comes bursting through the door one night after work.

He's gasping for breath and throws himself on the couch.

"What's wrong?" his wife asks. "Why are you so out of breath?"

"First give me a glass of water," he gasps.

His wife rushes to the kitchen and brings him a glass of water.

"So, what is the matter?" the wife asks.

"Today, I had a really big achievement," he says. "I ran behind the bus all the way from the office to here. I saved $1."

"You silly old fool," his wife says. "You should have run behind a taxi. You could have saved $10!"

Don't Listen to the News, Economists, Politicians or Other "Gurus"

One night, the Potato family sat down to dinner—Mother Potato and her three daughters.

Midway through the meal, the eldest daughter spoke up. "Mother Potato? I have an announcement to make."

"And what might that be?" said Mother, seeing the obvious excitement in her eldest daughter's eyes.

"Well," replied the daughter, with a proud but sheepish grin, "I'm getting married!"

The other daughters squealed with surprise as Mother Potato exclaimed, "Married! That's wonderful! And who are you marrying, Eldest daughter?"

"I'm marrying a Russet!"

"A Russet!" replied Mother Potato with pride. "Oh, a Russet is a fine tater, a fine tater indeed!"

As the family shared in the eldest daughter's joy, the middle daughter spoke up. "Mother? I, too, have an announcement."

"And what might that be?" encouraged Mother Potato.

Not knowing quite how to begin, the middle daughter paused, then said with conviction, "I, too, am getting married!"

"You, too!" Mother Potato said with joy. "That's wonderful! Twice the good news in one evening! And who are you marrying, Middle Daughter?"

"I'm marrying an Idaho!" beamed the middle daughter.

"An Idaho!" said Mother Potato with joy. "Oh, an Idaho is a fine tater, a fine tater indeed!"

Once again, the room came alive with laughter and excited planning for the future, when the youngest Potato daughter interrupted. "Mother? Mother Potato? Um, I, too, have an announcement to make."

"Yes?" said Mother Potato with great anticipation.

"Well," began the youngest Potato daughter with the same sheepish grin as her eldest and middle sisters before her, "I hope this doesn't come as a shock to you, but I am getting married, as well!"

"Really?" said Mother Potato with sincere excitement. "All of my lovely daughters married! What wonderful news! And who, pray tell, are you marrying, Youngest Daughter?"

"I'm marrying Dan Rather!"

"DAN RATHER?!" Mother Potato scowled suddenly. "But he's just a common tater!"

Please do not take the advice of common taters, whether they be on the TV or radio, for your financial advice.

Albert Einstein goes to heaven and meets three other new guests. He asks the first guest, a physicist, his IQ.

"196, sir," says the first.

"Excellent," says Einstein. "I look forward to talking about my theory of relativity with you."

Einstein asks the same question to the second, a school teacher. "150," says the second.

"Not bad," Einstein says. "We can discuss pressing problems of world justice and peace."

Einstein asks the third person the same question.

"75, sir," is the reply.

Einstein thinks for a minute, and then asks, "So, how do you think the economy will do next year?"

A man is walking along a road in the countryside when he comes across a shepherd and a huge flock of sheep. He tells the shepherd, "I will bet you $100 against one of your sheep that I can tell you the exact number in this flock."

The shepherd thinks it over; it's a big flock so he takes the bet. "973," says the man.

The shepherd is astonished, because that is exactly right. He says to the man, "OK, I'm a man of my word, take an animal." The man picks one up and begins to walk away.

"Wait," cries the shepherd. "Let me have a chance to get even. Double or nothing that I can guess your exact occupation." The man agrees.

"You are an economist for a government think-tank," says the shepherd.

"Amazing!" responds the man. "You are exactly right! But tell me, how did you deduce that?"

"Well," says the shepherd, "put down my dog and I will tell you."

The mayor and his wife are out for a walk and they come upon a construction site. "Hello, Rebecca!" yells one of the construction workers to the mayor's wife, and the mayor's wife waves hello in return.

Stunned, the mayor asks, "Rebecca, how do you know that man?"

"Well, before you and I met, I used to date him."

The mayor smirks, "It's a good thing I came along, or else you'd be married to a construction worker."

"No," ponders the wife, "if I had married him, he'd be the mayor."

Many times I am asked, "Larry, which is better for the stock market and investors, Democrats or Republicans?"

I answer, "Remember the root of the word "politics": *poly* meaning 'many' and *ticks* meaning 'blood suckers.'"

It is always followed by laughter. Once this laughter dies down, I explain it really doesn't matter. They all tend to screw it up somehow.

Folks, you can get pretty confused listening to the experts on TV and in the newspaper about how to invest. Have you noticed that they all have different opinions?

It reminds me of a friend of mine who had a date with a pair of Siamese Twins. I asked him if he had a good time.

He said, "well, yes and no."

Companies...

I read the other day in the Wall Street Journal that Enron and Mobil were going to merge due to the recent events at Enron. They are going to call the new company MORON.

As you know, the stock market has not been in the greatest shape lately. It seems that, because of current economic conditions, many companies are contemplating mergers and acquisitions.

Here are a few to keep an eye on:

1. Xerox and Wurlitzer: they're going to make reproductive organs.

2. Fairchild Electronics and Honeywell Computers: the new company would be Fairwell Honeychild.

3. Polygram records, Warner brothers and Keebler: the new company would be Poly-Warner-Cracker.

4. W.R.Grace Co., Fuller Brush Co., Mary Kay Cosmetics, and Hale Business Systems: the new company would be Hale, Mary, Fuller, Grace.

5. 3M and Goodyear: the new company would be mmm good.

6. John Deere and Abitibi-Price: the new company would be Deere Abi.

7. Honeywell, Imasco and Home Oil: the new company would be Honey, Im Home.

8. Denison Mines, Alliance and Metal Mining: The new company would be Mine All Mine.

9. Grey Poupon and Dockers Pants: the new company would be Poupon Pants.

10. Knott's Berry Farm and the National Organization For Women: the new company would be Knott Now.

11. Zippo Manufacturing, Audi, Dofasco and Dakota Mining: the new company would be Zip Audi Do-Da.

12. Kentucky Fried Chicken and Shick Razors: the new company would be the Chicken-Shick.

A friend asked an investor, "Does the fluctuating stock market bother you?"

The investor replied, "No, not really. I sleep like a baby."

"Really?" the friend marveled.

"Yes, I sleep for an hour, then I get up and cry for an hour."

If you bought $1,000 worth of Nortel stock one year ago, it would now be worth $49.

If you bought $1,000 worth of Budweiser (the beer, not the stock) one year ago, drank all the beer, and traded in the cans for the nickel deposit, you would have $79.

(Not really a joke, but true, so start drinking heavily.)

Death & Estate Planning

On estate planning and taking it with you...

There once was a rich man who was dying. While on his death bed, he tried to negotiate with God to allow him to bring his earthly treasures with him to heaven.

"God, please, I have worked so hard to accumulate all these riches. Can't I bring them along?"

"This is very unusual," said God, "but since you have been such a faithful steward, I will allow you to bring one suitcase."

The man immediately had a servant fill a large suitcase with gold bricks. Shortly thereafter, he died. When he arrived at the pearly gates, he was stopped by St. Peter.

"I'm sorry sir, but you know the rule — 'You can't take it with you.' You may enter, but the suitcase has to stay outside."

"But God told me I could bring one suitcase," the man protested.

"Well, if God says it's OK, but I still need to examine the contents before you enter."

St. Peter took the suitcase from the man, opened it, and, looking very puzzled, said to the man, "You brought pavement?"

A new business was opening and one of the owner's friends wanted to send him flowers for the occasion. They arrived at the new business site and the owner read the card, "Rest in Peace."

The friend who sent the flowers was furious and called the florist to complain. He told the florist of the obvious mistake and how angry he was.

The florist said, "Sir, I'm really sorry for the mistake. But rather than getting angry, understand a funeral is taking place where there are flowers with a note saying, 'Congratulations on your new location.'"

A man and his wife visit the doctor because the husband had been having some health problems.

After examining the man for over an hour, the doctor asks thean to go sit in the waiting room and the doctor calls the

"I'm afraid he does not have long to live. If you do the following, however, you can keep him alive indefinitely: make him a nice breakfast and dinner every day; cater to his every desire and whim; do not upset him—let him watch the TV shows he wants and put his needs first."

In the car, the husband turns to his wife, "What did the doctor say?"

Wife responds, "You're gonna die."

This 75-year-old woman had a vision one night, she saw and spoke to God. She asked him, "How much time do I have to live?"

He said, "You have 35 years left." So that whole year she had a ton of cosmetic surgery, she had a face lift, a tummy tuck, her nose reshaped, liposuction, she completely did herself over. She figured as long as she was going to live another 35 years she was going to look young again.

After all this was done, that same year she was hit by a car and was killed instantly. When she entered St. Peter's gate she walked over to God and said, "What happened? I thought you said I had another 35 years!"

God replied, "I DIDN'T RECOGNIZE YOU!"

I was helping a couple with their estate planning and they started to have this discussion...

The husband turns to his wife and asks if she would want to continue to live in their house if he died. She said she wanted to stay there forever. So, he asked her, if she were to get remarried, would her new husband also live in the house?

She replied if she did get remarried her new husband would live there, too.

So he asked about his car, his prized Corvette—would she let him drive the car?

She said if he needed to drive the car, he could drive it.

Taken aback by the way the conversation was going, the husband prepared himself to ask her the really big question: what about his golf clubs? She wouldn't let him use those, would she?

She said, "No, absolutely not! He's left-handed!"

I asked my son what he would like for Christmas.

He replied, "Power of Attorney."

Definition of perfect estate planning: You want your last check to bounce.

Possible closing for financial workshops...

Ladies and Gentlemen, I have outlined a number of common, costly financial mistakes most Retirees make, and shared a few safe and proven ways you can avoid these mistakes.

But, my friends, making these mistakes is not the real problem. The real problem is if you choose to do nothing about correcting or avoiding them...particularly when the opportunity to do so is so readily available to you. In other words...

You, and you alone, are the one who must now decide
Whether to act on this opportunity, or toss it aside.
You are the one who must now make up your mind
Whether you will reach out, or just linger behind;
Whether you will make use of these proven ways from afar
Or just be content to blindly stay where you are.
So, take it or leave it, I've given you something to do!
Just think it over...It's now all up to you!

Because, nobody here will compel you to be wise.
No one will force you to open your eyes.
But, if you refuse my help, and financial advice
Then you are the one who risks paying the price.
You must decide in the face of your financial quest
Whether to shirk this opportunity, or give it your best.
So, the selection is yours, whichever you do,

To be more successful with your money, is all up to you!

Procrastination has cost me great,
It only leads to sorrow,
It's a terrible habit I must break,
Perhaps I'll start tomorrow.

When asking a crowd to raise their hands based on their investment experience, I say, "Raise both hands if you are a top-notch investor."

This is the kind of person who wonders why he hasn't been invited to speak on CNBC.

The next level is a one-hander. This investor loves to talk about investments socially. In fact, the comment is often heard in his/her home: "Honey, can we talk about something else?"

Raise your hand half-way if you somewhat follow investments, but you get the Wall Street Journal mainly to impress your friends.

And, if you don't know the difference between a large cap, mid cap, and a hub cap, and if you think the S&P is the local grocery store, keep your hands down.

A woman wrote a letter to her stockbroker asking how the

market was doing. She received the following reply:

Helium is up and feathers are down. Paper remains stationary. Fluorescent tubing shares have dimmed in light trading. Knives are up sharply. Cows continue to steer into a bull market. Pencils are losing a few points.

The hiking equipment sector is trailing. Escalators are rising, while elevators continue their slow decline. Barbells are up in heavy trading. Light switches are off and shares of arrows are on target. Mining equipment is hitting rock bottom.

Diapers remain unchanged and shipping lines are staying at an even keel. The market for raisins is drying up and Pepsi Cola is fizzling. Toilets might tank and Caterpillar stock is inching up a bit.

Sun reached its peak at midday and balloon prices remain inflated. Scott Tissue continues to touch new bottoms and batteries are exploding in attempts to recharge the market.

When speaking about estate planning and charitable giving comes up...

Two friends are marooned on an island after their boat is destroyed during a storm.

The first man is frantic, he is ranting on the beach, "Oh no, they'll never find us, we're DOOMED!"

His friend is swimming around calmly in the blue waters enjoying himself.

"How can you be so calm? We are going to die!"

The calm friend responds, "I earned $50,000 my first year in business and gave 10% to charity. I earned $200,000 the next year and gave 10% to charity. This year I made $500,000 and haven't given yet. They'll find us!"

A young kid of six or seven had listened intently to the conversation at the dinner table with his visiting grandmother as the guest of honor. He could wait no longer to ask her. He interrupted, "Grandma, can you make a sound like a frog?"

She looked at him astonished, and said, "I don't think I can, but I'll try. Why?" she asked, confused.

He replied, "Because Dad says when you croak, we get $50,000."

A wealthy 86-year-old man, about to die, calls in his 3 trusted advisors: his CPA, attorney and priest.

He tells them, "I've decided I'm gonna take my money with me. I've liquidated my estate and placed $10 million in each of these 3 envelopes. Here's one for each of you and I ask that you each place the envelope in my casket at my funeral."

At the funeral, they each toss the envelope into the casket. Later, the CPA turns to the priest and says, "Did you really toss $10 million into the casket?"

"No I did not. That money can do so much good, I took it for the church and tossed in an empty envelope. I can't see how God can be mad with me."

The CPA says, "To tell the truth, I was having some business problems. I took out $200,000 to pay off some debts and get myself out of hot water."

"I can't believe you guys," says the astonished attorney. "Mr. Smith trusted us his whole life, more than he trusted his family, and you guys can't even honor his last wish?"

"Did you throw in the $10 million?" the CPA asks the attorney.

"You're darn right! The envelope contained my personal check!"

You can use the above story as a lawyer joke (Folks, you can't take it with you—if you try, it will wind up in the hands of an attorney), or to poke fun at any profession. Or you can have the three characters be the 3 children if you want to provide an analogy for an estate planning concept (e.g., never leave outright cash gifts to children).

Health Care

Three men are standing at the Pearly Gates. St. Paul asks the first one, "What did you do during your lifetime?"

The man says, "I found the cure for cancer, a disease that killed millions of people and affected nearly every member of my family."

St. Paul says, "Well, that is wonderful. Come on in." He asks the second man, "What did you do?"

The second man says, "I found the cure for AIDS, a modern plague that was thought to be incurable."

St. Paul says, "Wonderful. Come on in." He asks the third man, "What did you do?"

The third man says, "I invented the HMO. I saved many companies a lot of money."

St. Paul says, "Come on in, but you can only stay for three days."

Seems an elderly gentleman had serious hearing problems for a number of years.

He went to the doctor. The doctor was able to have him fitted for a set of hearing aids that allowed the gentleman to hear perfectly again.

The elderly gentleman returned to the doctor's in a month for a final check on the new equipment. After some tests, the doctor proclaimed, "Your hearing is perfect!"

"Thank you for helping me," replied the elderly man.

"You're welcome," said the doctor. "Your family must be really pleased that you can hear again."

"Oh, I haven't told them yet. I just sit around and listen to the conversations I used to miss," replied the elderly gentleman.

"Really!?" questioned the doctor. "You must still be marveling at being able to hear again and just not ready to believe it yourself. That must be why you haven't told them."

"Well, no, that's not it exactly...but I have changed my will three times!"

Everyone's in it for the Money

During a Papal audience, a businessman approached the Pope and made this offer: change the last line of the Lord's prayer from "Give us this day our daily bread" to "Give us this day our daily chicken" and KFC will donate $10 million to Catholic charities.

The Pope declined.

Two weeks later the man approached the Pope again, this time with a $50 million offer. Again the Pope declined.

A month later the man offers $100 million, this time the Pope accepts.

At a meeting of the Cardinals, the Pope announces his decision in the good news/bad news format. "The good news is... that we have $100 million for charities. The bad news is that we lost the Wonder Bread account!"

A man visiting a fishing resort stopped at the General Store to buy some beer. He was surprised to see the sign above the beer case reading "WARM BEER ONE DOLLAR MORE PER CASE."

The customer asked the owner of the store if the sign wasn't in error, since in his experience a store always charges more for the cold beer.

"No, the sign, is correct," replied the owner. "Customers were complaining that the beer I sold them was warm, and putting up the sign ended the complaints."

Costly Advice...

Two long-time friends, a doctor and a lawyer, are talking at a party. Their conversation is constantly interrupted by people describing their ailments, and asking the doctor for free medical advice.

At one point, the exasperated doctor asks the lawyer, "What do you do to stop people from asking you for legal advice when you're out of the office?"

"When they ask, I give it to them," replies the lawyer, "and then I send them a bill."

The doctor is shocked, but agrees to give it a try. The next day, still feeling slightly guilty, the doctor prepares the bills.

As he's finishing, his secretary brings in the day's mail. There on top — a bill from the lawyer.

You never know what happens when you make a charitable donation...

Father Michael opens a letter from a friend and a $20 bill falls out. As he reads the letter, he is distracted by the actions of a shabbily dressed man leaning against a post outside.

Fearing the man is in financial distress, the good priest takes the $20 bill, wraps it in a piece of paper on which he'd written "Don't Despair," and tosses it to the man outside.

The man picks it up, reads it, looks at the priest with a puzzled expression, tips his hat and walks away.

The next morning Father Michael is told a man is at the door asking for him. Downstairs, he finds the stranger who hands him a wad of money.

"What's this for?" the good priest asks.

"That's the 60 bucks you have coming. Don't Despair paid 6-1."

Some people just don't understand money.

Take the owner of the small clothing shop that was burglarized. A detective was questioning him about how much he lost.

"It's bad," said the proprietor, "but it's not as bad as it could have been if he'd robbed me yesterday."

"Why is that?" the detective asked.

"Because today everything was on sale."

Recently heard message on answering machine:

If you are…
the phone company: I already sent the money.
my parents: please send money.
my financial aid institution: you didn't lend me enough money.
my friends: you owe me money.

It can buy a house, but not a home.
It can buy a bed, but not sleep.
It can buy a clock, but not time.
It can buy you a book, but not knowledge.

It can buy you a position, but not respect.
It can buy you medicine, but not health.
It can buy you blood, but not life.
It can buy you sex, but not love.

So you see, money isn't everything and it often causes pain and suffering. I tell you this because I am your friend and as your friend I want to take away all of your pain.

So, please send me all your money and I will suffer for you. Cash only. Small bills.

A young man was walking through a supermarket to pick up a few things when he noticed an old lady following him around. Thinking nothing of it, he ignored her and continued on. Finally, he went to the checkout line, but she got in front of him.

"Pardon me," she said, "I'm sorry if my staring at you has made you feel uncomfortable. It's just that you look just like my son, who I haven't seen in a long time."

"That's a shame," replied the young man, "is there anything I can do for you?"

"Yes," she said, "as I'm leaving, can you say 'Good bye, Mother!' It would make me feel so much better."

"Sure," answered the young man.

As the old woman was leaving, he called out, "Good bye, Mother!"

As he stepped up to the checkout counter, he saw that his total was $127.50. "How can that be?" he asked, "I only purchased a few things!"

The clerk said, "Your mother said you would pay for her."

It was summer. Sales were way down. The independent discount store operator was frantic with worry. Wal-Mart had moved in down the street and now Target was opening less than a mile in the other direction. He went to his minister for help.

"What can I do?" he asked.

"Do you have a swimming pool?" asked the minister.

"Yes, I do."

"Good. Wait for a day when there is a nice breeze. Put on your swimsuit. Take this Bible and plop yourself down in a lounge chair alongside that swimming pool. Open the Bible at random and let the wind flip the pages for you. When the pages stop moving, look down at the book. The answer to your problem will be in what your eyes first light on."

The retailer thanked him and went away. A year passed. The same man drove up to the church office in a new Cadillac. He and his wife, who was glittering with jewelry, got out and went into the office and asked for the minister. The man was wearing a new Brooks Brothers suit and exuded prosperity.

"Do you remember me?" the man asked the minister. "I was here a year ago and you gave me some advice."

"How did it turn out?"

It solved all my problems and gave me a new start,"
enthused the man, handing the minister an envelope stuffed
with $100 bills.

"I'm glad I could help you. Tell me, what passage was it
that was so inspirational?"

"I did exactly what you told me," said the man. "I sat in the
lounge chair with the Bible open on my lap and let the wind
flip the pages. When they stopped moving, I looked
down."

"Yes, yes," said the minister, "but what did you read?"

"The first words I saw were 'Chapter 11.'"

Instant Gratification

A man and a woman walk into a very posh Rodeo Drive furrier. "Show the lady your finest mink!" the fellow exclaims.

So the owner of the shop goes in back and comes out with an absolutely gorgeous full-length coat. As the lady tries it on, the furrier sidles up to the guy and discreetly whispers, "Ah, sir, that particular fur goes for $65,000."

"No problem! I'll write you a check!"

"Very good, sir," says the shop owner. "Today is Saturday. You may come by on Monday to pick it up, after the check has cleared."

So the man and the woman leave. On Monday, the fellow returns. The store owner is outraged, "How dare you show your face in here?! There wasn't a single penny in your checking account!!"

"I just had to come by," grinned the guy, "to thank you for the most wonderful weekend of my life!"

In the middle of a talk:

"Listen closely. There are 3 simple rules for doubling your money every year. Unfortunately, I don't know what they are."

Use this only if you are good with gestures—this gets a good laugh if you can put a silly/stupid look on your face.

On talking about the younger generation, and how they do not save enough and they just want to buy a BMW:

"The problem with immediate gratification is that it takes too long."

A profound philosophy of this "New Age" was reflected in the last will and testament of a once rather wealthy man. It read: "Being of sound mind, I spent most of my money on cars, boats, fine food and good whiskey. I also spent a good bit of it on women. What was left, I spent foolishly."

A very successful businessman had a meeting with his new son-in-law.

"I love my daughter, and now I welcome you into the family," said the man. "To show you how much we care for you, I'm making you a 50-50 partner in my business. All you have to do is go to the factory every day and learn the operations."

The son-in-law interrupted, "I hate factories. I can't stand the noise."

"I see." replied the father-in-law. "Well, then, you'll work in the office and take charge of some of the operations."

"I hate office work," said the son-on-law. "I can't stand being stuck behind a desk all day."

"Wait a minute," said the father-in-law. "I just made you half-owner of a moneymaking organization, but you don't like factories and won't work in a office. What am I going to do with you?"

"Easy," said the young man. "Buy me out."

Pete and Gladys were looking at a new living room suite in the furniture store.

Pete says to the salesman, "We really like it, but I don't think we can afford it."

The salesman says, "You just make a small down payment... then you don't make another payment for six months."

Gladys wheeled around with her hands on her hips and said "Who told you about us?"

"Hello, Mr. Brown," said the sales rep. "I'm calling because our company replaced all the windows in your house with our triple-glazed weather-tight windows over a year ago, and you still haven't sent us a single payment."

Mr. Brown replied, "But you said they'd pay for THEMSELVES in 12 months."

A manager told an applicant applying for a job, "I can start you at $7 an hour and in three months up that to $10/hr. When do you want to start?"

The applicant responded, "In three months."

Not What it Seems

Investors often have misconceptions about financial topics. When they learn all of the facts, however, they realize their misconceptions. The stories below are excellent illustrations.

This guy is stranded on a desert island, all alone for ten years. One day, he sees a speck in the horizon. He thinks to himself, "It's not a ship." The speck gets a little closer and he thinks, "It's not a boat." The speck gets even closer and he thinks, "It's not a raft." Then, out of the surf comes this gorgeous blonde woman, wearing a wetsuit and scuba gear.

She walks up to the guy and says, "How long has it been since you've had a cigarette?"

"Ten years!" He says. She reaches over and unzips a waterproof pocket on her left sleeve and pulls out a pack of fresh cigarettes. He takes one, lights it, takes a long drag, and says, "Man, oh man! Is that good!"

Then she asked, "How long has it been since you've had a drink of whiskey?"

He replies, "Ten years!"

She reaches over, unzips her waterproof pocket on her right sleeve, pulls out a flask and gives it to him.
He takes a long swig and says, "Wow, that's fantastic!"

Then she starts unzipping the long zipper that runs down the front of her wet suit and she says to him, "And how long has it been since you've played around?"

The man cries, "My God! Don't tell me you've got golf clubs in there, too!"

A depressed young woman was so desperate, that she decided to take her own life by throwing herself into the ocean.

When she went down to the docks, a handsome young sailor saw her tears, took pity on her, and said, "Look you have a lot to live for. I'm off to Europe in the morning, and if you like, I can stow you away on my ship. I'll take good care of you and bring you food every day." Moving closer he puts his arm around her and added, "I'll keep you happy and you'll keep me happy."

The girl nodded yes and thought what did she have to lose? That night, the sailor brought her aboard and hid her in a lifeboat. From then on, every night he brought her three sandwiches and a piece of fruit, and they made passionate love all night.

Three weeks later, during a routine search, she was discovered by the captain. "What are you doing here?" the captain asked.

"I have an arrangement with one of the sailors; he's taking me to Europe."

"Europe, Madam?" said the captain, "this is the Staten Island ferry."

Two men are walking their dogs in the park on a sunny Sunday morning. One man turns the other and says, "What a beautiful morning. Let's go across the street and have some breakfast."

"Good idea, but have you forgotten? We've got the dogs."

"Don't worry about that, just follow me."

With that they head off to the café and the first man puts on his sunglasses and opens the door.

The doorman stops him and tells him that he can't come in; pets are not allowed due to health regulations.

The man interjects, "But he's my seeing eye dog. I'm blind."

The doorman agrees and allows the man into the café. The second man takes a deep breath and decides to try his luck.

He crosses the street, puts his sunglasses on and sidles up to the café. Once again the doorman stops him at the door and explains that he can't let him in because of the dog.

"But this is my seeing eye dog."

"Hang on a minute, your dog's a Chihuahua!"

"What? Those jokers gave me a Chihuahua?!"

Another story about substance vs. form, or you can use this a few minutes after telling a joke.

"Thanks for laughing at that story… I'm not really a good storyteller. In fact, you may have heard about the man in prison…"

A new inmate at the prison is surprised during dinner when one of the convicts stands up and says, "24," and all of the other prisoners laugh hysterically. Another stands up and says "315," with the same results. "You see," explains one of the prison veterans, "we only have one joke book here, and everyone knows the jokes by heart. Instead of telling the entire joke, we just give the number of the joke from the book."

The new prisoner waits a few days, then stands up at dinner and says, "73." No one laughs. "What's wrong?" he asks the veteran.

"Must be your delivery." (Shrug your shoulders and grimace.)

A Day Off!

The other day, my assistant had the nerve to ask for an extra day off, so I explained it to her:

So you want the day off. Let's take a look at what you are asking for:

There are 365 days per year available for work.
There are 52 weeks per year in which you already have two days off per week,
Leaving only 261 days available for work.

Since you spend 16 hours each day away from work you have used up 170 days,
Leaving only 91 days available.

You spend 30 minutes each day on coffee break that accounts for 23 days each year.
Leaving only 68 days available.

With a hour lunch period each day,
You have used up another 48 days
Leaving only 22 days available for work.

You normally spend 2 days per year on sick leave.
This leaves you only 20 days available for work.

We offer 5 holidays per year,

So your available working time is now down to 15 days.
We generously give you 14 days vacation per year.
Which leaves you only 1 day available for work —

I'll be damned if you're going to take that day off!

A man wakes up from a 20-year coma.

He immediately calls his broker. "Excellent! My IBM is
worth $6 million! And my Microsoft is worth $8 million!"

As he is asking about his AOL stock the operator cuts in
and says "Please deposit another $3 million for the next 3
minutes."

Rich man...

A young lad was asking a rich, elderly gentleman how he
had made his fortune.

The old guy fingered his worsted wool vest and said this:
"Well, son, it was 1932 — the depth of the Great
Depression. I was down to my last nickel. I invested that
last nickel in an apple. I spent the entire day polishing the
apple and, at the end of the day, I sold the apple for 10
cents."

"I then invested that 10 cents in two apples," the old guy continued. "I spent the next day polishing them and sold them for twenty cents. I continued this system for a month, by the end of which I'd accumulated a fortune of $1.37."

"Then, my wife's father passed away and left us $2 million dollars."

A journalist assigned to the Jerusalem bureau has an apartment overlooking the Wailing Wall. Every day when she looks out, she sees an old bearded man praying devoutly. Certain he would be a good interview subject, the journalist goes down to the Wailing Wall, and introduces herself to the old man.

She asks, "You come every day to the Wall. Sir, how long have you done that and what are you praying for?"

The old man replies, "I have come here to pray every day for 25 years. In the morning, I pray for world peace and for the brotherhood of man. I go home, have a cup of tea, and I come back and pray for the eradication of illness and disease from the earth. And very, very important, I pray for peace and understanding between Israelis and Palestinians."

The journalist is impressed. "How does it make you feel to come here every day for 25 years and pray for these wonderful things?" she asks.

The old man replied, calmly, "Like I'm talking to a wall."

A woman walked up to a little old man rocking in a chair on his porch.

"I couldn't help noticing how happy you look," she said. "What's your secret for a long, happy life?"

"I smoke three packs of cigarettes a day," he said. "I also drink a case of whiskey a week, eat fatty foods, and never exercise."

"That's amazing," the woman said. "How old are you?"

"Twenty-six." he said.

A well-dressed drunk who smelled like a martini sat down on a subway seat next to a Priest. The man's tie was stained, and a half-empty bottle of gin was sticking out of his coat pocket. He opened his Wall Street Journal and began reading.

After a few minutes, the man turned to the Priest and asked, "Say, Father, what causes arthritis?"

"My son, it's caused by loose living and too much alcohol."

"Well, I'll be darned," The well-dressed drunk muttered, returning to his Wall Street Journal.

The Priest, feeling bad about what he had said, nudged the man and apologized. "I'm very sorry. I didn't mean to come on so strong. How long have you had arthritis?"

"Oh, I don't have arthritis, Father. I was just reading here that the Pope does."

Insurance

A man walks into an insurance office and asks for a job. "We don't need anyone," they replied.

"You can't afford not to hire me," he argued. "I can sell anyone anything anytime."

"Fine. We have two prospects that no one has been able to sell. If you can sell just one, you have a job." They hand him the paperwork and out he goes. He was gone about two hours. When he returned, he handed them two checks, one for $25,000 and another for $50,000.

They were amazed. "How in the world did you do that?" they asked.

"I told you I'm the world's best salesman, I can sell anyone anything, anytime."

"Did you get a urine sample?" they asked him.

"What's that?" he asked.

"Well, if you sell a policy over $20,000, the company requires a urine sample. Take these two bottles and go back and get urine samples."

He was gone about 8 hours and they were preparing to close when in he walks with two five gallon buckets, one in each hand. He sets the buckets down, reaches in his shirt pocket, produces two bottles of urine on the desk and says, "Here's Mr. Brown's, and this one is Mr. Smith's."

"That's good," they said, "but what's in those two buckets?"

"Well, I passed by the schoolhouse and they were having a state teachers convention. I sold them a group policy!"

An insurance salesman was calling people on the phone. He was new and not very bright.

He says, "Mr. Jones, my name is Art Mortell, and I'm calling to sell you some life insurance."

The man on the phone responds, "I have all I need."

The salesman asks, "How much do you need?"

"$10,000," says the man.

The salesman says, "I guess you're not planning on being dead very long."

A farmer's barn burns down, so he calls the insurance company to collect.

The adjuster from the insurance company comes out, inspects the burned farm, and explains to the farmer how they will rebuild it for him.

The farmer says, "No, I really don't want my barn rebuilt. I'm getting older and I would rather just have the $50,000 it's insured for."

The adjuster explains, "That's not the policy of our company. We replace the damaged item. We do not give cash."

"I don't see what difference it makes," says the farmer. "It costs you $50,000 either way. Just give me the cash," demands the farmer.

Again, the adjuster replies, "That's not company policy."

"In that case," says the farmer, "cancel that life insurance policy I have on my wife."

A life insurance company which prided itself on efficiency, sent one of its agents out to see the widow Murphy the day after her husband's funeral.

Judging everything to be in order, the agent produced a check for $50,000 and presented it to the widow.

Mrs. Murphy was quite overcome, and it took several minutes before she could get ahold of herself. "You know," she sobbed, "Murphy was such a GOOD husband. Why, I'd give $15,000 of this to have him back right now."

Life insurance agent to would-be client: "Don't let me frighten you into a hasty decision. Sleep on it tonight. *If* you wake in the morning, give me a call then and let me know."

"You ought to feel highly honored," said the businessman to the life insurance agent. "So far today I've had my secretary turn away seven insurance agents."

"Yes, I know," replied the agent, "I'm them."

An elderly couple went to a doctor. They told the doctor, "We're having some trouble with our sex life. Could you watch and offer some suggestions?"

The doctor replied, "I'm not a sex therapist. You should find someone else."

The couple said, "No, no, we trust you."

After watching them have sex, the doctor said, "You don't seem to be having any troubles. I wish my sex life was as good. I can't give you any suggestions."

This was repeated the next week and also the third week. After they had finished on the third week, the doctor said, "You aren't having any trouble. Is this your idea of kinky sex?"

The man replied, "No, actually the problem is if we have sex at my house, my wife will catch us. If we have sex at her house, her husband will catch us. The motel charges us $50, and we can't afford that. You only charge $35, and Medicare pays half of that."

On introducing life insurance:

I met a guy yesterday working on immortality. He told me so far, so good.

Long-term care insurance:

An old man living in California had lived a very good life and was granted one wish by God.

The man was afraid to fly, and he had always wanted to go to Hawaii. So, he asked God to build him a road to Hawaii.

God replied that would be very hard to do. Did he have any other wishes?

The man asked God to explain long-term care insurance to him.

God replied: "How many lanes do you want?"

A pregnant patient, upon having a conversation with her doctor, learns that her insurance policy covers parts but not labor.

Keeping Things in Perspective (After a Market Decline)

You've got to keep things in perspective and not focus on the short run.

There's a lesson that can be learned from the farmer who got into an accident. He was in his horse and carriage riding along the road with his dog, when he got hit by a truck. Within minutes a police officer arrived.

The police officer took one look at the horse, saw that it had been maimed and said, "I should put this horse out of its misery." He pulls his gun out and shoots him. On his way over to help the farmer, he comes across the dog, barely breathing and the officer says, "I've got to have compassion for this dog and his condition—he'll never make it." He pulls out his gun again and shoots him.

He finally gets over to the farmer who is pinned beneath the Mack truck and asks, "Are you okay?"

"I feel great!" exclaims the farmer.

One day, a diver was enjoying the aquatic world 20 feet below sea level.

He noticed a guy at the same depth, but he had no scuba gear on whatsoever.

The diver went down another 20 feet, and the guy joined him a few minutes later.

The diver went down another 25 feet, and minutes later, the same guy joined him.

This confused the diver, so he took out a waterproof chalkboard set, and wrote, "How the heck are you able to stay under this deep without equipment?"

The guy took the board and chalk, erased what the diver had written, and wrote, "I'm drowning, you moron!"

A client of mine came into my office recently with a note from his daughter who just recently went away to college. He asked me if he could share the note with me because he was very upset and wanted my opinion.

He took out the note and began to read:

"Dear Dad, I wanted to drop you a quick note to tell you everything is fine at school, but I decided to move in with my boyfriend, Joe. After we finish school, we are going to get married and move in with Joe's parents in Alaska."

As he is reading this note from his daughter, my client is getting very agitated. I couldn't believe what I was hearing.

After he finished the note, I noticed there was a "P.S." at the bottom of the letter. I took the note, and it said, "P.S. Dad, please forgive me. All of the above is not true — I made it up. I got a 'D' in chemistry, and I wanted to put it in proper perspective."

Well, folks, that's exactly what I want to do this evening— put things in their proper perspective for you in light of the current volatile market.

Winston Churchill used to give lectures to students at Oxford.

One morning, in a social sciences class, he glared at his wide-eyed students and asked, "What part of the human anatomy can grow up to TEN times its normal size when exposed to external stimuli?"

A pretty young girl in the front row sheepishly blurted out, "The male penis?" Churchill abruptly and rather loudly cut her off, "WRONG! Anyone else?"

A bookish young man raised his hand and offered, "The pupil in the human eye expands and contracts when exposed to different levels of light. The total surface area in dim light can be ten times that when exposed to bright light."

"Correct!" said Churchill. He turned to the female student and said sternly, "Young lady, from your response I gather you did not do your reading, AND you are doomed to a life of excessive expectations!"

Lawyers, Accountants, and Other Professions

Did you hear the news today? Apparently, there's a terrorist holding a room full of lawyers at gunpoint down at the courthouse. He swears he'll release one every hour until his demands are met.

An actuary is someone who studied to be a CPA, but didn't have the personality for it.

The attorney and his two friends, the Jewish CPA and his Hindu doctor are camping for the weekend. They get lost, it's getting dark and cold and they come upon a farmhouse.

They knock on the door and explain their problem to the farmer.

The farmer invites them to stay the night but explains that he only has room enough for two of them to sleep in the house. One needs to stay in the barn. The doctor volunteers to stay in the barn and everyone goes to bed.

Twenty minutes later, there's a knock at the front door. The farmer opens the door and the Hindu doctor says, "I'm sorry, I cannot stay in the barn. There is a cow in there and cows are sacred to my people. I cannot stay there in the presence of the sacred animal." The CPA volunteers to stay out in the barn and gives the doctor his bed in the house.

Twenty minutes later these a knock at the door. The farmer opens the door and there stands the Jewish CPA. "I cannot stay in the barn. There is a pig there. Pigs are unclean animals to my people and I cannot sleep there." The attorney agrees to trade places with the CPA.

Twenty minutes later, there is a knock at the door. The farmer opens the door and there stand the cow and the pig.

At a country club party, a young man was introduced to an attractive girl. Immediately, he began paying her court and flattering her outrageously. The girl liked the young man, but she was taken aback by his fast and ardent pitch. She was stunned when, after 30 minutes, he seriously proposed marriage.

"Look," she said. "We only met a half hour ago. How can you be so sure? We know nothing about each other."

"You're wrong," the young man declared. "For the past 5 years I've been working in the bank where your father has his account."

Actuaries...

A financial planner and two actuaries walk into a restaurant.

Once seated, the waiter approaches the financial planner and asks, "what will you have for dinner this evening?"

The Financial Planner responds, "I think I'll have the prime rib."

The waiter says, "and for your vegetables?"

The financial planner empathetically looks at his two actuary friends and says, "Oh, they'll have prime rib, too."

Economists are great. They have accurately predicted 14 of the last 4 recessions.

Joe: "The last time I visited Times Square in New York, I was totally amazed by the large number of actuaries' daughters who came right up to me and said, 'Hello there, big guy.'"

Jim: "That's very interesting, Joe, but how did you know they were all actuaries' daughters?"

Joe: "Because, without hesitation, every single one of them immediately stated her cash surrender value."

Frank, the financial genius, was opening his new office. As he sat there wondering where to put the pencil holder, a fellow walked through the door.

Frank wanted to look busy, so he picked up the phone and pretended to be talking to a client. He motioned to the man in his office to hold on a moment.

"Yes, I can see you about your financial plan," Frank said into the phone. "No, I can't see you this week, but perhaps next Thursday. No, not in the morning, two-thirty is the only time I have left. Yes, two-thirty would be fine. I'll see you then."

Frank hung up the phone, made a note in his planner and turned to the fellow standing in front of his desk. "Now, sir, what can I do for you?"

"Nothing," the man said. "I'm just here to install that phone."

Lawyers...

(Two boys on a playground)

Boy 1: "What does your dad do?"

Boy 2: "He's a lawyer."

Boy 1: "Honest?"

Boy 2: "No, the regular kind."

A Compliance Officer was giving a presentation to his registered reps.

Two minutes into the presentation, someone yells from the back of the room "I can't hear you back here!"...at which point everyone moves to the back of the room.

A Human Resources manager had trouble getting a gentleman to sign up for his 401(k).

He wanted 100% participation, so finally, after several months, he called the gentleman into his office and said, "You either sign up for your 401(k) or you're fired."

The man immediately signed up on the spot.

The Human Resources manager was surprised at how easy it was, and asked, "Why did you sign up so freely today?"

To which the employee answered, "I just never had anyone explain it as well as you did."

A large company was holding a national convention for their sales representatives.

On the first morning, the Vice President of Marketing announced that one of their longtime sales representatives, Joe, had become ill during the night and passed away.

At noon, Joe's good friend, Bill, also a representative, talked to the VP and found out that Joe was at the local funeral home down the street waiting to be shipped home. They agreed to go and pay their respects after the meeting.

Later on, as they were leaving the funeral home, and Bill said to the VP, "I can't believe it. . . Joe looked terrible. What in the world did he have?"

The VP said, "North and South Dakota."

My first job was working in an orange juice factory, but I got canned. Couldn't concentrate.

After that I tried to be a tailor, but I just wasn't suited for it, mainly because it was a sew-sew job.

Then I tried to be a chef — I figured it would add a little spice to my life, but I just didn't have the "thyme."

Next I tried working in a muffler factory, but that was too exhausting.

I managed to get a good job working for a pool maintenance company, but the work was just too draining.

I attempted to be a deli worker, but any way I sliced it, I couldn't cut the mustard.

Then I worked in the woods as a lumberjack, but I just couldn't hack it, so they gave me the ax.

Next was a job in a shoe factory. I tried, but I just didn't fit in.

So then I got a job in a workout center, but they said I wasn't fit for the job.

After many years of trying to find steady work, I finally got a job as an historian until I realized there was no future in it. I studied a long time to become a doctor, but I didn't have any patients.

My best job was being a musician, but eventually I found I wasn't noteworthy.

I became a professional fisherman, but discovered that I couldn't live on my net income.

My last job was working at Starbuck's, but I had to quit because it was always the same old grind.

SO I RETIRED, AND FOUND I'M PERFECT FOR THE JOB!

Memory Loss

Two senior couples are walking along, wives in front, husbands in back. Herb says to Sam, "Gee, we went to a new restaurant last night and had the best meal ever. Good prices too."

Sam says, "Well, we like to eat out, too. What was the name of the restaurant?"

Herb says, "You're going to have to help me out here a little. What's the name of that pretty flower, smells sweet, grows on a thorny bush?"

Sam says, "How about 'rose'?"

"Yes, yes, that's it!" cries Herb. He calls ahead to his wife: "Rose. Hey, Rose! What was the name of the restaurant we ate at last night?"

Three elderly gentlemen were standing and talking after dinner. One man said that he was having trouble with his memory. "Just yesterday I found myself in front of the refrigerator with a jar of mayonnaise in my hand. I had no idea if I had just gotten it out of the fridge to put some on my sandwich or if I had just put some on my sandwich and was about to put it back in the fridge."

"I know just what you mean," said the second gentleman. "I was standing at the bottom of the stairs with a book in my hand. I could not remember if I had just brought it down to read or if I was finished reading and about to take it back upstairs and put it away."

The third elderly gentleman, who was the host, said, "I am fortunate that I have not had that kind of problem, knock on wood," as he knocked three times on the table. Then he looked up and said, "Excuse me, I think I hear someone at the door."

When speaking about aging, especially to a retirement crowd, (or if you simply forget something), you can ask the audience or your prospect if they ever forget anything (you will get a big agreement):

By the way, does anyone here ever notice that you forget some things? I'm sure it's nothing compared to a client I had...

I'm walking in the park one day and I see my client, a 90-year-old man, sitting on a park bench, sobbing. I stop and ask him what is wrong.

Through his tears the old man answers, "I'm in love with a 25-year-old woman."

"What's wrong with that?" I asked.

Between the sobs and sniffles, he answers, "You can't understand. Every morning before she goes to work, we make love. At lunchtime, she comes home and we make love again, and then she makes my favorite meal. In the afternoon when she gets a break, she rushes home and loves me again, the best an old man could want. And then at supper time, and all night long, we make love." He breaks down, no longer able to speak.

I put my arm around him and say, "I don't understand. It sounds like you have a perfect relationship. Why are you crying?"

The old man answers, sobbing, "I forgot where I live!"

An elderly husband and wife noticed that they were beginning to forget many little things around the house. They were afraid that this could be dangerous, as one of them may accidentally forget to turn off the stove and cause a fire. So, they decided to go and see their physician to get some help.

Their physician told them that many people their age find it useful to write themselves little notes as reminders. The elderly couple thought this sounded wonderful, and left the doctor's office very pleased with the advice.

When they got home, the wife said, "Dear, will you please go to the kitchen and get me a dish of ice cream? And why don't you write that down so you don't forget?"

"Nonsense," said the husband. "I can remember a dish of ice cream!"

"Well," said the wife, "I'd also like some strawberries on it. You better write that down, because I know you will forget."

"Don't be silly," replied the husband. "A dish of ice cream and some strawberries. I can remember that!"

"Ok, dear, but I'd like you to put some whipped cream on top. Now you'd really better write it down. You will forget," said the wife.

"Come now, my memory's not all that bad," said the husband. "No problem, a dish of ice cream with strawberries and whipped cream." With that, the husband shut the kitchen door behind him.

The wife could hear him getting out pots and pans, and making some noise inconsistent with his preparing a dish of ice cream, strawberries, and whipped cream. He emerged from kitchen about 15 minutes later.

Walking over to his wife, he presented her with a plate of bacon and eggs.

The wife took one look at the plate, glanced up at her husband and said, "Hey, where's the toast?"

There was this man who was down on his luck and felt he needed a few drinks. He went to this bar and drank several drinks, when he was done he stood up and walked toward the door. The bartender shouted at the man, "Hey, mister, are you going to pay for those drinks?"

The man looked back at the bartender and replied, "I already paid you," then walked out the bar.

Almost immediately, he saw one of his friends and told him about the bartender, "Just go in there and drink all you want, then get up and leave. When the bartender asks you to pay the tab, just tell him you already did."

This sounded easy enough, so he went in and had several drinks. The bartender went to him and said, "Before you came in, another man was here before you, and when I asked him to pay his tab he told me he already did, but I don't remember him paying me."

The man replied, "I would love to stay and hear your story but I don't have time. Can I have my change, please?"

A guy was invited to some old friends' home for dinner. His buddy preceded every request to his wife by endearing terms, calling her "Honey," "My Love," "Darling," "Sweetheart," "Pumpkin," etc.

He was impressed since the couple had been married almost 70 years, and while the wife was off in the kitchen he mentioned this to his buddy:

"I think it's wonderful that after all the years you've been married, you still call your wife those pet names."

His buddy hung his head. "To tell you the truth," he said, "I forgot her name about ten years ago."

SENILITY PRAYER
God, grant me the Senility
To forget the people
I never liked anyway,
The good fortune
To run into the ones I do,
And the eyesight
To tell the difference.

Folks, if you hear a good idea, write it down. Don't trust your memory...

A nice couple on a long road trip stop to have lunch. They're back on the road, when about 30 miles down the highway the wife says, "Oh, my goodness, I forgot my glasses at the diner."

Well, ladies, you know most of us fellas don't like to stop to use the restroom when we're on the highway, much less drive 30 miles out of the way.

So, he's not too happy, and he's giving her the business all the way back to the diner: "Honey, how could you forget your glasses?" — "Of all the silly things!" — " What were you thinking?"

Well, they finally get back to the diner. As she's walking to the door he rolls down his window and says " Honey, while you're in there, you might as well get my hat."

Marriage

A successful man is one who makes more money than his wife can spend. A successful woman is one who can find such a man.

Marriage is a three ring circus: an engagement ring, a wedding ring, and suffering.

Before marriage, a man yearns for the woman he loves. After marriage, the "y" becomes silent.

It's best to use a piece a paper and write the word "yearns" as you say it, then cover the "y" as you finish."

Love is blind, but marriage is an eye-opener.

The man approached a very beautiful woman in a large supermarket and asked, "You know, I've lost my wife here in the supermarket. Can you talk to me for a couple of minutes?"

"Why?" She asks.

"Because every time I talk to a beautiful woman, my wife appears out of nowhere."

When I got married, my mother-in-law gave my wife good advice. She told her, "Always remember that the man is the head of the family," (as you smirk) "but the woman is the neck — she tells the head look here, look there." (Take your head in both hands and turn it left, and then right).

I have a client who told me his ex-wife used to blame me every time he bought a stock and it would go down. One night they were stopped in the car by a policeman.

He comes over to the car and says to my client, "You were speeding."

"Geez," he says, "I didn't realize it."

"You did, too, and I told you two miles back," bellows his wife. (Roll your eyeballs)

"Be quiet!" he says to her.

"You also have a broken tail light and you're not wearing a seat belt. I will have to cite you for those, too," says the officer.

"I told you," said his wife.

By now he was infuriated with his wife and snaps, "Shut up!"

"Does he always talk to you like that, ma'am?" asked the officer.

She replies, "Only when he's been drinking!"

At the end of seminars, my evaluation forms double as a lottery ticket and this increases the number of forms I receive (and appointments that I close). Or, if you mention striking it rich, say something about winning the lottery:

Speaking of lotteries — reminds me of some clients of mine. The husband was in the garage and his wife was in the living room watching television late on a Saturday afternoon. She was watching the state lottery drawings. Suddenly, he hears her start screaming and he rushes in from the garage and sees her jumping up and down on the sofa.

"What's the matter?" he asks.

"Nothing's the matter, I just won $2 million in the lottery! Go pack, Harry, go pack!"

He runs upstairs and pulls out the suitcases for vacation. He walks half way back down the stairs and asks his wife, "Should I be packing warm clothes for a cold weather vacation or light clothes for warm weather?"

She says, "Harry, pack all your clothes and be out by noon tomorrow!"

Two drunks are sitting on a park bench. The first one says to the second, "How did you reach this low point in your life?"

Second replies, "I was married to a woman that I adored. I gave her whatever she asked for. The more I gave her the more she wanted. I had a good job and, out of necessity, started working 10 to 12 hours a day. I went to work on Wall Street to make even more money and worked longer hours. No matter what I did or how much I gave her it wasn't enough. One night when I came home, the house was empty. The note said she ran off with someone who made more money. That's when I started drinking and wound up here."

Second asks First, "How did you reach your low point in life?"

First replies, "I think I'm the one who ran off with your wife."

Ask your audience, "Who makes the investment decisions in your house? Is it the husband or wife?"

When I was very young, my dad told me that my mom made all the decisions. In fact, one day after school, my dad picked me up from school to take me to a dental appointment.

Knowing the parts for the school play were supposed to be posted that day, he asked me if I'd gotten a part. I enthusiastically announced: "Yeah, Dad...I'll be playing the part of a man who's been married for twenty years."

He said, "Congratulations! That's great, son. Keep up the good work and before you know it, they'll be giving you a speaking part."

A couple returns from their honeymoon, and it's obvious to everyone that they are not speaking to each other. The groom's best man takes him aside and asks what is wrong.

"Well," replied the groom, "when we had finished making love on the first night, I got up to go to the bathroom and I put a $50 bill on the pillow without thinking."

"Oh, I wouldn't worry about that too much," said his friend. "I'm sure your wife will get over it soon enough."

The groom nodded gently and said, "That may be true, but I can't get over the fact that she gave me $20 change!"

I have a client whose wife does not trust him with money. Actually, she just doesn't trust him...

Last week, he went to the bar with his friends after work. They started drinking heavily and he met a woman there who was looking for some companionship. One thing led to another, they went back to her place, and you can guess what happened.

At three o'clock in the morning, he wakes up and cries, "Oh God! My wife will kill me! Do you have any baby powder? Rub it on my hands."

A little perplexed, the woman gets the baby powder and rubs it on his hands.

At four o'clock in the morning, he walks in the front door of his house and his wife is sitting in the living room chair waiting. "Where have you been?" she demands.

"Well, I went for some drinks with some of the guys, I met a woman at the bar, I went back to her place, and one thing led to another."

"Let me see your hands," she demands. As she looks at his hands, she exclaims, "You've been bowling, haven't you?!"

The retired attorney, who resides in a very beautiful neighborhood, was out on his front lawn gardening.

A brand new, shiny Mercedes pulls up. A well-dressed, well-to-do looking woman steps out and says to the attorney, "This garden is absolutely beautiful. How much do you charge?"

"Nothing," replies the attorney. "The woman in the house lets me sleep with her."

Ad seen in the newspaper last week...

FOR SALE BY OWNER

Complete set of Encyclopedia Britannica. 45 volumes. Excellent condition. $1,000 or best offer. No longer needed. Got married last weekend. Wife knows everything.

All my sons married good housekeepers.
When they got divorced, the wives got to keep the house.

The bride, white of hair
stood over her cane.
Her footsteps, uncertain,
need guiding...
While across the church aisle,
the bridegroom, in wheelchair,
comes a riding...

Now, who is this elderly couple thus wed?
Well, you'll find when you've closely explored it...

That here is that rare, extraordinary pair...
Who waited 'til they could afford it!

There was a woman who had been married to four different men with four diverse occupations.

Her friend asked her why she had first married a banker, then an actor, then a clergyman and finally a mortician.

She responded: "One for the money, two for the show, three to get ready and four to go."

"If you'll make the toast and pour the juice, sweetheart," said the newlywed bride, "breakfast will be ready."

"Good. What are we having for breakfast?" said the new husband.

"Toast and juice," she replied.

A woman awoke during the night to find her husband was not in bed. She put on her robe and went downstairs.

He was sitting at the kitchen table with a cup of coffee in front of him. He appeared to be in deep thought, just staring at the wall. She saw him wipe a tear from his eye, then take a sip of his coffee.

"What's the matter, dear? Why are you down here at this time of night?" she asked.

"Do you remember twenty years ago when we were dating, and you were only 16?" he asked.

"Yes, I do," she replied.

"Do you remember when your father caught us in the back seat of my car making out?"

"Yes, I remember."

"Do you remember when he shoved that shotgun in my face and said, 'Either you marry my daughter or spend the next twenty years in jail?'"

"Yes, I do," she said.

He wiped another tear from his cheek, and said, "You know...I would have gotten out today."

A husband and wife were shopping. "Darling, it's my mother's birthday tomorrow," the wife said. "What shall we buy for her? She would like something electric."

The husband replied, "How about a chair?"

A young man excitedly tells his mother he's fallen in love, and is going to get married.

He says, "Just for fun, Ma, I'm going to bring over three women, and you try and guess which one I'm going to marry."

The mother agrees.

The next day, he brings three beautiful women into the house and sits them down on the couch and they chat for a while. He then says, "Okay, Ma, guess which one I'm going to marry."

She immediately replies, "The one in the middle."

"That's amazing, Ma. You're right. How did you know?"

"I don't like her."

How many people notice that when you read the paper, everyone else's stocks seem to be rising except yours. You wish you had the other stocks...

It reminds of the woman who went to the police station with her next-door neighbor to report that her husband was missing.

The policeman asked for a description. She said, "He's 35 years old, 6 foot 4, has dark eyes, dark wavy hair, an athletic build, weighs 185 pounds, is soft-spoken, and is good to the children."

The next-door neighbor protested, "Your husband is 5 foot 4, chubby, bald, has a big mouth, and is mean to your children."

The wife replied, "Yes, but who wants HIM back?"

The Yuppette had married a stockbroker.

When asked how they met, she replied, "Oh, we were introduced by a *Mutual Fund.*"

Sadie's husband, Jake, has been slipping in and out of a coma for several months, yet his faithful wife stays by his bedside day and night.

One night, Jake comes to and motions for her to come closer.

He says, "My Sadie, you have been with me through all the bad times. When I got fired, you were there to support me. When my business failed, you were there. When I got shot, you were by my side. When we lost the house, you gave me support. When my health started failing, you were still by my side. You know what, Sadie?"

"What, dear?" she asked gently.

"I think you're bad luck."

I was bickering with my wife the other day.

I said, "Honey you're so darn argumentative, you always disagree. As a matter of fact, if I said something was white, you'd probably say it was black just to disagree, wouldn't you?"

She says, "No."

One-Liners

Work to live, live to love, love to shop — so you see, if I can buy enough things, I'll never have to work at love again!

A journey of a thousand miles begins with a cash advance.

It's not hard to meet expenses — they're everywhere.

I've been shopping for 20 years, and I still don't have anything to wear.

If you look good and dress well, you don't need a purpose in life.

Let's go shopping — I need the exercise.

I'm so broke, I can't even pay attention.

I belong in a home for the terminally billed.

Living life to its credit limit.

I met a very young, intelligent man yesterday. I say he was young and intelligent, as he was about my age and agreed with everything I said.

Before beginning a talk:

I will keep my comments today brief and to the point. I learned this lesson when I heard a book report from a six-year-old boy, who wrote about Socrates. His book report read:

> Socrates lived a long time ago.
> Socrates gave long speeches.
> Socrates' friends poisoned him.

When giving a talk, someone voices an opinion or point of view that's negative or pessimistic (e.g., but the stock market has got to fall any day now…). I reply:

"It's all in the way you think about it. Science says that you become what you think about all day long. For instance, I have a friend who's becoming a woman."

Henny Youngman once came to one of my seminars. He comes up to me at the end and says, "Larry, that was a very nice talk. But money doesn't concern me. I have all I need—so long as I die by 4 pm!"

The fastest way to double your money: fold it over and put it back in your pocket.

I read that drinking too much is bad for your health, so I gave up reading.
— Henny Youngman

Has anyone here ever had the experience of a bad investment? Now you know the definition of experience. Experience is what you get when you don't get what you want.

I'm particularly keen on Irish investments. It's because their capital is always Dublin.

Have you heard the expression money talks?
Unfortunately, the only thing most people have ever heard it say is "goodbye."

Why do they call it "take-home" pay? Because that's as far as you can go with it.

Just remember this on estate planning: Where there's a will, there's a relative.

My first boss in an accounting firm told me there are only two kinds of people who hate income taxes: Men and women.

A coin comes up heads 10 times, and quits to become a day trader.

I can only please one person a day. Today is not your day. Tomorrow is not looking good, either.

All those who believe in telekinesis, please raise my hand.

I plan to live forever. So far, so good.

Did you hear they are making a movie about the recent accounting scandal? They are going to call it *Take the Money Enron*.

A thief stuck a pistol in a man's ribs and said, "Give me your money!"

The gentleman, shocked by the sudden attack, said, "You can't do this, I am a congressman!"

The thief said, "In that case, give me *my* money!"

Did you know that seniors are the largest carrier group of AIDS? That's right, Rolaids, Band-aids, government aids, Medicaid, hearing aids, etc.

There's something much bigger than money. Bills.

Running into debt isn't so bad. It's running into creditors that hurts.

We have the highest standard of living in the world. Too bad we can't afford it.

I'm working for a good cause...
Cause I need money.

I love my job, it's the work I hate.

Business is so bad, even the people who don't pay have stopped buying.

He is so rich, he has an unlisted phone *company*.

I like to read. The last book I bought was on Enron.
I'm up to Chapter 11.

"You put ten grand in a bank for one year at 5 percent and
what do you get?"

"A toaster."

"The best way to keep money in perspective is to have
some."
—Louis Rukeyser

"I spend money with reckless abandon. Last month I blew
five thousand dollars at a reincarnation seminar. I got to
thinking, what the hell, you only live once."
—Ronnie Shakes

What this country needs is a bank where you deposit a
toaster and they give you $250.

Banks are really pushing savings accounts. A bandit robbed
a bank of $2,000 the other day, and the teller tried to talk
him into opening into an IRA.

I once went golfing with my banker, but never again. Every time I yelled "FORE!" he yelled "CLOSURE!"

"I hear the bank is looking for a cashier."
"Thought they just hired one a week ago?"
"That's the one they're looking for."

Lots of banks are failing. I haven't been worried until recently I went in to ask about a loan, and they said, "Great! How much can you loan us?"

I never knew why banks called them "personal loans." I missed three payments and, boy, did they get personal!

Be careful of those calendars banks give you to help you keep track of your payments. I saw one with 16 months on it.

You can tell when you're in trouble—the bank sends somebody to repossess your toaster.

They now have a microwave bank—it's for those who want to go through their money faster.

I was a cashier in a bank for a while, but then I went on to something else.

What was that? Jail.

A young college grad applied for a job with a bank. The personnel officer asked, "What kind of job do you want?"

"I'll take vice-president for a start."

"We already have 12 vice presidents."

"That's OK. I'm not superstitious."

One bank opened a branch near a cemetery. In the window, the president put a sign that read, "You can't take it with you when you go, but here's a chance to be near it."

It's unfortunate that the person who writes the bank's advertising doesn't also approve the loans.

Banks lend billions to Third World countries, but for us, they chain down the pens.

Many smaller banks have gone through reorganization after discovering that they had more vice presidents than depositors.

A senior loan officer was standing by the desk of a junior loan officer when the telephone rang.

The junior officer answered, saying, "No...no...no...no...yes...no," and hung up.

The senior officer questioned him immediately. What had he said "yes" to?

"Don't worry, " said the junior officer reassuringly. "I said 'yes' only when he asked me if I was still listening."

Bank robber went up to teller and said "Stick 'em down."

The teller said, "Don't you mean Stick 'em Up?"

The bank robber said, "No wonder I'm not making any money."

Question: Where does Santa Claus put all of his money?

Answer: In the snow bank.

Question: Do you know who was the first financial person listed in the Bible?

Answer: The Pharaoh's daughter — she went to the river and took out a little prophet!

Coffee...

The coffee in our office is so bad that Dr. Jack Kevorkian recommends it to all his patients.

The coffee in our office is so strong that you can have it by the cup or by the slice.

A new employee came into our office and said, "I'd love to have a cup of coffee."
Someone asked, "One lump or two?"
She said, "I don't take sugar.
The employee said, "Who said anything about sugar?

I've got so many coffee stains on my desktop, Juan Valdez

wants to buy it for his museum.

Retirement...

This is the time when your spouse finally finds out what your co-workers have been putting up with for years.

Here at the company you had supervisors, managers, executive managers, vice-presidents, and a CEO. At home, you'll just have your spouse. Now you'll learn what following orders really means.

Racehorses are retired to stud. Unfortunately, that's not one of the options on our pension plan.

I cleaned my desk once and found three employees we thought had retired.

The last time I cleaned my desk, the stuff was so old I just threw it all out...although I did sell 6 magazines to my doctor for his waiting room.

"I'm a walking economy," a man was overheard to say. "My hairline's in recession, my waist is a victim of inflation, and together they're putting me in a deep depression."

A study of economics has revealed that the best time to buy anything is…last year!

On the day of my retirement, I told my spouse, "I'm home for good."

She said, "You're home. The 'good' part remains to be seen."

I said to my wife, "What can I do to help around the house?"

She said, "Ask for your old job back."

I told the boss that, during my retirement, I plan to be more active than I've ever been.

He said, "I imagine you would have to be."

When you retire, you switch bosses — from the one who hired you to the one who married you.

While reviewing his portfolio, an investor is watching the evening news.

The anchor says, "the recovery is just another quarter away!"

"I hope so," says the investor, "because that's what I'm down to!"

Unfortunately, after the markets' performance the past two years, most peoples' 401(k)s are now 201(k)s.

What's the definition of an accountant?

Someone who solves a problem you didn't know you had in a way you don't understand.

What's the definition of a good tax accountant?

Someone who has a loophole named after him.

When does a person decide to become an accountant?

When he realizes he doesn't have the charisma to succeed as an undertaker.

What's an extroverted accountant?

One who looks at your shoes while he's talking to you instead of his own.

What's an auditor?

Someone who arrives after the battle, and bayonets all the wounded.

Why did the auditor cross the road?

Because he looked in the file and that's what they did last year.

How do you drive an accountant completely insane?

Tie him to a chair, stand in front of him and fold up a road map the wrong way.

What do accountants suffer from that ordinary people don't?

Depreciation.

Definitions...

Definition of estate planning: "orderly conversion of wealth into commissions & fees." Seriously, it's when two people enter into a relationship where one has dollars and the other has knowledge, which ultimately results in their roles being reversed.

Bull Market: A random market movement causing an investor to mistake himself for a financial genius.

Bear Market: A 6 to 18-month period when the kids get no allowance, the wife gets no jewelry and the husband/wife gets no sex.

"Buy, Buy": A flight attendant making market recommendations as you step off the plane.

Standard & Poor: Our life in a nutshell.

Stock Split: When your ex and his/her lawyer split all your assets equally between themselves.

Cash Flow: The movement our money makes as it

disappears down the toilet.

Day Trader: Someone who is disloyal from 9-5.

Cisco: Sidekick of Pancho.

Yahoo!: What we yell after selling it to some poor sucker for $240 per share.

Windows 2000: What we jump out of when we're the sucker that bought Yahoo! for $240 a share.

Profit: Religious guy who talks to God.

Bill Gates: Where God goes for a loan.

Stock: A magical piece of paper that is worth $33.75 until the moment you buy it. It will then be worth $8.50.

Bond: What you had with your spouse until you pawned his/her golf clubs to invest in Amazon.com.

Broker: The person you trust to help you make major financial decisions. (Please note the first five letters of this word spell b-r-o-k-e.)

Bear: What your trade account and wallet will be when you take a flyer on that hot stock tip your secretary gave you.

Bull: What your broker uses to explain why your mutual funds tanked during the last quarter.

Margin: Where you scribble the latest quotes when you're supposed to be listening to your manager's presentation.

Short Position: A type of trade where, in theory, a person sells stocks he doesn't actually own. Since this also only ever works in theory, a short position is what a person usually ends up being in (i.e., "The rent, sir? Ha, ha, ha, well, I'm a little short this month.").

Commission: The only reliable way to wake money on the stock market, which is why your broker charges you one.

Yak: What you do into a pail when you discover your stocks have plunged and your broker is making a margin call.

S:\Systems\SEMINARS\Sixways\Program
Folders\CD\Compliance Versions\Securities America

Patience

When talking about having patience in the stock market:

Speaking about patience reminds me of the young man who decided to become a monk. So he chose a monastery that had one rule: you could only say two words every 10 years.

After 10 years the senior monk calls him in and says, "What do you have to say for yourself?"

The younger monk thinks and says, "Bed hard."

Another 10 years pass and the younger monk, now middle aged, is called up again and asked what he wants to say. Again, he thinks and says, "Food cold."

Another 10 years pass and the monk is called in once again. The now very senior monk says to the younger monk, "Well, what do you have to say?"

The younger monk replies, "I quit!"

"Doesn't surprise me a bit," says the senior monk. "You've been complaining ever since you got here."

A man steps out of his door to get the newspaper one morning. Looking down he sees a snail sitting there not doing a thing, just poking along. He bends over, picks up the snail and throws the little guy as hard and as far as he can.

Three years go by, and the man hears a knock at his door. Opening the door he looks out and then down to see the snail. The snail asks, "Why did you do that?"

Parenting

A man walked into a cigar store and asked for a 25 cent cigar. The man behind the counter commented, "Your son comes in here and buys 50 cent cigars."

The reply was, "The difference is he has a rich father."

As I grow older with my children, I am starting to realize something about God. God is an acronym for "Good Old Dad."

A father had been trying to teach his teenage son the value of money. One afternoon, he saw the perfect opportunity:

Son: "Hey Dad, can I borrow fifty dollars?"

Dad: "Forty dollars! What do you need thirty dollars for? Here's twenty."

Poverty is catching. You can get it from your kids.

A young woman brings her fiancé home to meet her parents. After dinner, her mother tells her father to find out about the young man, so the father invites the fiancé to his study for a drink.

"So what are your plans?" the father asks the young man.

"I am a Torah scholar," he replies.

"A Torah scholar. Hmmm," the father says. "Admirable, but what will you do to provide a nice house for my daughter to live in, as she's accustomed to?"

"I will study," the young man replies, "and God will provide for us."

"And how will you buy her a beautiful engagement ring, such as she deserves?" asks the father.

"I will concentrate on my studies," the young man replies. "God will provide for us."

"And children?" asks the father. "How will you support children?"

"Don't worry, sir. God will provide," replies the fiancé.

The conversation proceeds like this, and each time the father questions, the young idealist insists that God will provide.

Later, the mother asks, "How did it go, honey?"

The father answers, "He has no job and no plans, but the good news is he thinks I'm God."

For seminars, make a transparency of this letter:

The letter to Dad from college:

Dear Dad,

$chool i$ really great. I am making lot$ of friend$ and $tudying very hard.

With all my $tuff, I $imply can't think of anything I need, $o if you would like, you can ju$t $end me a card, a$ I would love to hear from you.

Love,
Your $on.

The reply:

Dear Son,

I kNOw that astroNOmy, ecoNOmics, and oceaNOgraphy are eNOugh to keep even an hoNOr student busy.
Do NOt forget that the pursuit of kNOwledge is a NOble task, and you can never study eNOugh.

Love,
Dad

Regarding teaching children lessons—about money, etc.

A young boy had just gotten his driving permit. He asked his father, a minister, if they could discuss the use of the car.

His father took him to his study and said to him, "I'll make a deal with you. You bring your grades up, study your Bible a little, and get your hair cut, and we'll talk about it."

After about a month the boy came back and again asked his father if they could discuss use of the car. They again went to the father's study where his father said, "Son, I've been real proud of you. You have brought your grades up, you've studied your Bible diligently, but you didn't get your hair cut!"

The young man waited a minute and replied, "You know Dad, I've been thinking about that. You know, Samson had long hair, Moses had long hair, why, even Jesus had long hair."

His father replied, "Yes, and they *walked* everywhere they went!"

Teacher: "If you had one dollar and you asked your father for another, how many dollars would you have?"

Vincent: "One dollar."

Teacher (sadly): "You don't know your arithmetic."

Vincent (sadly): "You don't know my father."

Mrs. O' Henry was talking to her husband one night about their son and his allowance.

"Well, darling," said Mr. O' Henry, "I had a long talk with him last week about the value of a dollar."

"I know," she replied, "the other day he asked for his allowance in Yen."

Self-Effacing Humor

It's always a good idea to start a seminar or talk with some self-effacing humor. It shows the audience that you are a real person who can laugh at yourself.

Folks, please let me know if I start talking too fast today, or if I confuse you. It all started when I took a speed-reading course last year.

Before the course, I was reading 200 words per minute with 98% comprehension. I now read 1,000 words per minute with no comprehension.

Good morning. My name is Larry Klein. As you may have seen from the information in your packets, I have been in the financial business for many years. I'm a Certified Financial Planner, a CPA, and I have an MBA from Harvard, which means I left a whole bunch of tuition money in Boston.

I need to tell you what happened, and why I do not practice as a CPA any more. I came home from work one evening and found that the sink in the kitchen was all stopped up. Not being particularly mechanical, I called the plumber, who arrived promptly. He fixed the problem and was packing up his tools, ready to leave. I asked him how much I owed him. Now, this was in 1979, and he says I owe him $100.

"$100!" I exclaimed. "You were only here 20 minutes! I'm a CPA and I don't even charge $100 an hour."

He says, "Neither did I when I was a CPA!"

You can use the above with most any prior profession you had or make up one for the humor—e.g., "Most people don't believe that I used to be a neurosurgeon—let me tell you what happened..."

To show the value of hiring a professional...

A large manufacturing company was having a problem with one of their crucial pieces of equipment. They tried everything. They called in all of their specialists, and still their expensive piece of equipment was sitting there worthless.

Finally, they called one of their recently retired engineers and offered to pay him a consulting fee. He arrived early one morning and looked over the equipment. He studied the machinery all day. Finally, at the end of the day, he placed a chalk "X" mark on the machinery and told them to replace that part.

Sure enough, the machinery started and ran flawlessly. Management was ecstatic and asked the engineer how much they owed him. Needless to say, they were surprised to see his bill was $20,002. They demanded an itemized bill.

The engineer wrote on a piece of paper:

"One Chalk "X": $2
"Knowing where to put it: $20,000."

A great way to open a seminar presentation...

The last time I gave this talk a lady came up to me, all excited, wanting to pay me a compliment. "Oh, Doug," she said, "That was the most inspiring presentation I've ever heard!"

"Why thank you very much," I replied. "I'm thinking of having it published posthumously."

"Oh, Doug," she said. "The sooner the better!"

"Before we get started, I would like to know how many people here tonight believe in reincarnation?"

I paused and stared at those who lift their hands, then said, "good to see you again."

A Harvard study was done on the relationship between an audience and the speaker at a financial seminar.

The psychology department found that one-third of the audience would be able to follow and understand the speaker's presentation, which is good news for me (the speaker).

The bad news is that the second third could not care less. They have been dragged out by their spouse, and are there for the food and drink.

However, the most interesting part of the study was the last third of the audience. They found that during the presentation, they would be having their own personal fantasies.

So, it is very comforting for me (the speaker) to know that AT LEAST A THIRD OF YOU will have a good time here.

This is a great story to tell at seminars because it shows that you are human, and that you can laugh at yourself. But it also helps people remember your name. Frequently, when I call a client and say "John, this is Stewart Fleisher" they will say, Well, *BON APPETIT!*"

Now, I know communication is important. I first realized that when I was a teenager, we were on a ship traveling to Europe, and I had to sit next to a Frenchman for dinner. As we sat down to eat, the Frenchman said "Bon Appetit."

Well, I was just a teenager and didn't speak any French. I thought he was introducing himself, so I stood up and said "Stewart Fleisher" and shook his hand. That happened several nights in a row.

Finally, a friend of mine pulled me aside and said to me that when the Frenchman said "Bon Appetit" he was not introducing himself, but saying "good appetite — hope you enjoy your meal." I felt really stupid.

So, the last night as I sat down, I said "Bon Appetit" and the Frenchman jumped up and said "Stewart Fleisher" and shook my hand.

Upon receiving a nice introduction, say:

The last time I gave a talk, the introducer reminded the audience that if you can't say something nice about someone don't say anything at all…"Please welcome our next speaker, Larry Klein."

Stockbrokers

A minister dies and is waiting in line at the Pearly Gates. Ahead of him is a guy who's dressed in sunglasses, a loud shirt, leather jacket, and jeans.

Saint Peter addresses this guy, "Who are you, so that I may know whether or not to admit you to the Kingdom of Heaven?"

The guy replies, "I'm Joe Cohen, stockbroker, of Noo Yawk City."

Saint Peter consults his list. He smiles and says to the stockbroker, "Take this silken robe and golden staff and enter the Kingdom of Heaven."

The stockbroker goes into Heaven with his robe and staff, and it's the minister's turn. He stands erect and booms out, "I am Joseph Snow, pastor of Saint Mary's for the last forty-three years."

Saint Peter consults his list. He says to the minister, "Take this cotton robe and wooden staff and enter the Kingdom of Heaven."

"Just a minute," says the minister. "That man was a stockbroker, he gets a silken robe and golden staff. How can this be?"

"Up here, we work by results," says Saint Peter. "While you preached, people slept; his clients, they prayed."

My broker and I are working on a retirement plan. Unfortunately it's *his*.

Two stockbrokers are on a hunting trip and they get lost. They stumble upon a farmhouse who is inhabited by a young woman living alone. They ask to spend the night and are permitted to do so.

Nine months later, one of the brokers, Ted, gets a letter from the woman's attorney.

Ted takes the letter and walks into John's office. "Do you remember that hunting trip we went on nine months ago?"

Looking a little sheepish, John replies, "Yes?"

"Remember that woman who let us stay in her farmhouse?" "Yes?" John replies.

"Did you sleep with her and tell her that you were me?"

"I'm sorry, Ted," John says full of repentance.

"That's okay. Her lawyer wrote me. She died suddenly and left her entire $2 million estate to me!"

If you want to poke fun at the stock market or if you are selling against it (e.g., convincing people that annuities are better):

I really didn't know much about the stock market until I was a senior in college. Here's what happened.

There was this guy, Ed, in my dormitory the entire 4 years of college. He was the genius type. He had these thick Coke-bottle glasses and never went to class—but he always got A's on every test. Instead of going to class, he just sat in his room and studied the stock market. He had stock charts all over the walls and even had a computer before you could buy them in a store!

Upon reaching my senior year, I realized it was time to get serious, that I would need to go out and make some money. So I went down to talk to Ed.

"Ed," I said, "I'll work as hard as I have to. Tell me how I can make $1 million dollars in the stock market."

He pondered a minute, lowered his head, looked at me over the top of those thick glasses, and said, "Start with $2 million."

Here's a nice way to knock the prospect's current stockbroker, advisor or financial planner...

A stockbroker died and went to Heaven. However, he was met at the pearly gates by St. Peter and the Devil.

St. Peter said, "Today, Mr. Stockbroker you are a lucky person. You have a choice to make. You have the opportunity to visit Heaven and Hell and decide where you would like to spend eternity."

The stockbroker thought for minute and said, "I have always heard how bad Hell is, so I guess I will go there first."

Immediately, the Devil snapped his fingers and he and the stockbroker were in Hell. The stockbroker was amazed. It wasn't at all what he had imagined. The most beautiful golf courses, sandy beaches, and pretty women were everywhere he looked; everything he imagined Heaven to be.

He got so caught up in enjoying the beauty and entertainment, he spent nearly three months in Hell. He finally realized that he had a choice to make so he summoned the Devil and they went back to the pearly gates and met St. Peter.

The stockbroker said, "St. Peter, I know what a good time

I have been having, so I can't wait to see Heaven." St. Peter snapped his fingers and immediately they were in Heaven.

The stockbroker looked around in dismay. There were only little puffs of clouds with angel-type figures on them strumming harps or just looking ethereal. The stockbroker thought to himself, "This isn't exactly what I thought Heaven would be. It won't take me long to decide." The stockbroker summoned St. Peter and they went back to the pearly gates.

The stockbroker said, "Heaven was not what I thought it would be, and Hell was everything I expected Heaven to be. Therefore, I choose to spend eternity in Hell."

Immediately, the Devil snapped his fingers and the stockbroker was back in Hell. This time though, he was buried up to his chin in dung, crows were picking his skin and eyeballs, and fire and brimstone was everywhere.

In a panic, the stockbroker yelled for the Devil and said, "The other day when I was here there were golf courses, sandy beaches, beautiful women and it was nothing like this."

The Devil replied, "The other day you were a prospect; today you're a client."

The stockbroker's secretary answered his phone one morning.

"I'm sorry," she said, "Mr. Bradford's on another line."

"This is Mr. Ingram's office," the caller said. "We'd like to know if he's bullish or bearish right now."

"He's talking to his wife," the secretary replied. "Right now, I'd say he's sheepish."

A stockbroker was cold calling about a penny stock and found a taker.

"I think this one will really move," said the broker, "and it's only $1 a share."

"Buy me 1,000 shares." said the client.

The next day the stock was at $2. The client called the broker and said, "You were right… give me 5,000 more shares."

The next day the client looked in the paper and the stock was at $4. The client ran to the phone and called the broker, "Get me 10,000 more shares," said the client.

"Great!" said the broker.

The next day the client looked in the paper and the stock was at $9. Seeing what a great profit he had in just a few days, the client ran to the phone and told the broker, "Sell all my shares!"

The broker said, "To whom? You were the only one buying that stock."

Mr. Client comes in for an appointment with his broker to review the performance of his account.

His broker begins the appointment by saying, "If you think money is the root of all evil, do I have great news for you!"

The ideal investment advisor has gray hair and hemorrhoids: gray hair to look distinguished, and hemorrhoids to look concerned!

Two people are sitting in a broker's office.

One of them stands up and yells across the desk between them:

"You don't understand! I need to liquidate those those B-shares today. My oldest kid starts college next week, my youngest needs braces, and I'm already behind on my mortgage. I need cash now! We can reinvest the money next month into A-shares!"

The other person then promptly stands and calmly says:

"I can understand your position. But, after taking a look at the situation, I don't believe that strategy is the best investment decision. Also, you told me you would not make any investment moves without my reviewing it first. After all, I *am* the client."

Taxes

A little boy wanted $100 badly and prayed for two weeks, but nothing happened. Then he decided to write God a letter requesting the $100. When the postal authorities received the letter addressed to God, USA, they decided to send it to the President.

The President was so impressed, touched, and amused that he instructed his secretary to send the little boy a $5 bill. The President thought this would appear to be a lot of money to a little boy.

The little boy was delighted with the $5, and sat down to write a thank you note to God, which read:

"Dear God, Thank you very much for sending the money. However, I noticed that for some reason you had to send it through Washington, D.C. and, as usual, those jerks deducted $95.00!"

Golf is alot like taxes. You drive hard to get to the green and then wind up in the hole.

Last Halloween one kid showed up at my door dressed as an IRS agent. It was very authentic. He took 40% of our candy.

A delicatessen owner was being audited by the IRS. The deli owner asked, "What's wrong? Why am I being audited?"

The IRS auditor replied, "You've got two trips to Europe down as business expenses. What's your explanation?"

The deli owner replied, "We deliver!"

I want to join a violent, armed group with no regard for the law... but the IRS isn't hiring.

The stockbroker received notice from the IRS that he was being audited.

He showed up at the appointed time and place with all his financial records, then sat for what seemed like hours as the accountant pored over them.

Finally, the IRS agent looked up and commented, "You must have been a tremendous fan of Sir Arthur Conan Doyle."

1040 Xtra EZ To Do Tax Form

a. How much money did you make this year? $_____
b. SEND IT IN.

What's the favorite tree of the IRS?

Eucalyptus ("You clipped us")

Do you know how the IRS feels about your money?

If you put "THE IRS" into one word and say it you will get the answer. (ANSWER= THEIRS)

The local bar was so sure that its bartender was the strongest man around that they offered a standing $1,000 bet.

The bartender would squeeze a lemon until all the juice ran into a glass, and hand the lemon to a patron. Anyone who could squeeze one more drop of juice out would win the money. Many people had tried over time (weightlifters, longshoremen, etc.) but nobody could do it.

One day a scrawny little man came into the bar, wearing thick glasses and a polyester suit, and said in a tiny, squeaky voice: "I'd like to try the bet."

After the laughter had died down, the bartender said OK, grabbed a lemon, and squeezed away. Then, he handed the wrinkled remains of the rind to the little man.

The crowd's laughter turned to total silence as the man squeezed the lemon, and 6 drops fell into the glass.

As the crowd cheered, the bartender paid the $1,000, and asked the little man, "What do you do for a living? Are you a lumberjack, a weightlifter, what?"

The man replied, "I work for the IRS."

Technology

A computer manufacturer called his bank and informed the loan officer that he needed an extension on his loan.

The loan officer said, "We need it today. We can't wait till next Monday."

The manufacturer asked, "Were you ever in the computer business?"

"No."

"You will be next Monday."

A guy walks into a bar and starts dialing numbers like a telephone on his open hand, then puts his palm up against his cheek and begins talking.

Suspicious, the bartender walks over and tells him this is a very tough neighborhood and he doesn't need any trouble here.

The guy says, "You don't understand. I had a phone installed in my hand because I was tired of carrying the cellular."

The bartender says, "Okay, buddy, prove it."

The guy dials up a number and hands his hand to the bartender. The bartender talks into the hand and carries on a conversation. "That's incredible!" says the bartender. "I would never have believed it!"

"Yeah," said the guy, "I can keep in touch with my broker, my wife, you name it. By the way, where is the men's room? I've gotta send a fax..."

Order Form

400 Greatest Jokes
and Audio CD

Give *400 Greatest Jokes* to a friend who is not funny so they can get their own copy and CD. Or, order now for an early Christmas gift!

The total price of **$39.95** includes:
- *400 Greatest Jokes*
- CD of Well-Told Jokes and *The Three Most Important Ingredients in Getting a Good Laugh*

To order:
Call (800) 980-0192; or fax this order to (925) 935-5991; or mail check or money order to:
NF Communications, Inc.
1700 N. Broadway #405
Walnut Creek, CA 94596

Name_____

Firm_____

Address_____

City_____State_____ZIP_____

Phone_____Fax_____

Email Address_____

Payment:
☐ Cashier's Check or Money Order
☐ Credit Card
Type_____Account#_____
Expiration Date_____

Signature_____

Information Request

I would like information on the programs checked below:

☐   Raise $1 Million Per Month with Seminars.

☐   How I Sell Two to Four Annuities a Month ($100,000+ Average) with Two Inexpensive Ads.

☐   LTC Seminar - The Road to Packing the Seminar Room with Senior Investors.

☐   Sell LTC Policies Hand Over Fist With This Simple Advertising System

☐   Generating Appointments with Your Prospecting Newsletter.

☐   Dow Dividend Strategy—Here's How to Beat 83% of equity Mutual Funds, Clients Will Flock to You.

☐   Estate Planning Seminar—Attract New Affluent Clients.

☐   Mechanical Money Management System.

☐   Become an Author Overnight—Have Your Own Book Published Overnight and Get Instant Credibility.

☐   How to Become a Fee-Based Advisor and Double Your Income.

☐   Public Relations Kit—How To Get Interviewed in the Newspaper Two to Four Times a Year and Get Well-Known in Town.

☐   Want to Close More Sales? This Video Presentation Program shows you how to scientifically close more sales.

☐   How to Attract a Ton of 401(k) Rollovers

☐   Client Leveraging System—Turn 100 Clients into 500

Name_____

Firm_____

Address_____

City_____State_____ZIP_____

Phone_____Fax_____

Email Address_____

Fax this request form to (925) 935-5991